HOLT McDOUGAL

Psychology
Principles in Practice

HOLT McDOUGAL
a division of Houghton Mifflin Harcourt

ISBN-13: 978-0-55-402691-6
ISBN-10: 0-55-402691-0

5 6 7 8 9 2266 18 17 16 15 14 13 12
4500371538

CONTENTS

Introduction and Teaching Strategies 1

Bibliography 2

Chapter 1, Reading 5
Ethical Principles of Psychologists and Code of Conduct, 2003

Chapter 2, Reading 7
King Solomon's Ring, Konrad Lorenz

Chapter 3, Reading 9
My Father Forgets, Lynn McAndrews

Chapter 4, Reading 11
Artificial Reality II, 2nd Ed., Myron W. Krueger

Chapter 5, Reading 13
Some Must Watch While Some Must Sleep, William C. Dement

Chapter 6, Reading 15
Apprenticeship in Thinking, Barbara Rogoff

Chapter 7, Reading 17
Witness for the Defense, Elizabeth Loftus and Katherine Ketcham

Chapter 8, Case Study 19
Understanding Children, Jerome Kagan

Chapter 9, Reading 21
"The IQ Puzzle," Sharon Begley

Chapter 10, Case Study 23
The Development of Imagination, David Cohen and Stephen A. MacKeith

Chapter 11, Reading 25
Endangered Minds, Jane M. Healy

Chapter 12, Reading 27
"Work and Family Relationships," Patricia Voydanoff

Chapter 13, Case Study 29
The Unresponsive Bystander, Bibb Latané and Jon M. Darley

Chapter 14, Reading 31
The Roots of the Self, Robert Ornstein

Chapter 15, Reading 33
"The Upper Limits of Ability Among American Negroes," Martin D. Jenkins

Chapter 16, Case Study 35
Who Will Raise the Children? James A. Levine

Chapter 17, Reading 37, 38
"Faces," essay by Terry Atkin Belanger
"Faces," essay by Jennifer Yeo

Chapter 18, Reading 39
Darkness Visible, William Styron

Chapter 19, Case Study 41
The Quiet Therapies, David K. Reynolds

Chapter 20, Reading 43
Psychology, William James

Chapter 21, Reading 45
The Saturated Self, Kenneth J. Gergen

Answers to Questions 47

READINGS AND CASE STUDIES

Introduction and Teaching Strategies

Readings and Case Studies is a collection of two-page excerpts from a variety of sources. The purpose of this collection is to help students broaden their base of sources of psychological information.

Overall, the excerpts provide a range of reading that reflects human diversity and varies in difficulty, style, and tone. Classic sources, such as William James' *Psychology* and Konrad Lorenz's *King Solomon's Ring,* are included, as well as very informal pieces, such as the essays on faces by Terry Atkin Belanger and Jennifer Yeo. The Readings and Case Studies in this booklet are directly related to chapter topics in the student's text. There is one Reading or Case Study for each chapter.

A list of all sources from which excerpts have been taken appears in the Bibliography section, which begins on page 2. A few of the excerpts include internal references. When this occurs, a note after the last question about the excerpt informs readers that information for cited references can be found in the Bibliography section. Information for all cited references within an excerpt appear under the title entry.

FORMAT All Readings and Case Studies reflect the following general format.

▶ **INTRODUCTION** Each Reading or Case Study begins with a short introduction that provides a context for the upcoming excerpt. This section ties the excerpt to the chapter topic, introduces the book or periodical from which the excerpt comes, and often gives some information about the author(s).

▶ **EXCERPT** Each excerpt—Reading or Case Study—is taken from a published work.

▶ **QUESTIONS** The final element in each Reading or Case Study consists of questions that require students to analyze what they have read, draw conclusions, make predictions, or formulate generalizations based on the knowledge gained from their reading. Sample answers to questions begin on page 47.

TEACHING STRATEGIES After reading an excerpt, many students will be interested in reading more from the source. If possible, have one or more copies of the book or periodical from which an assigned Reading or Case Study is taken available for student use. Allow time for students who do further reading to relate the excerpt to the rest of the piece. You may also wish to gather other books and articles by the selection authors.

Give students the opportunity to discuss the Readings or Case Studies in small groups or as a class. Ask students if each Reading or Case Study supports the other information they have about the same topic.

BIBLIOGRAPHY

American Psychological Association. (2003). *Ethical Principles of Psychologists and Code of Conduct*. Washington, DC: Author.

Begley, S. (1996, May 6). The IQ puzzle. *Newsweek*, pp. 70-72.

Belanger, T. A. (1996, June). Readers write: Faces. *The Sun: A Magazine of Ideas*, pp. 32-33.

Cohen, D., & MacKeith, S. A. (1991). *The development of imagination: The private worlds of childhood* (pp. 40-41, 51-52). London: Routledge.
Reference cited in excerpt
Flavell, J. H., Flavell, F. R., & Green, F. L. (1987). Young children's knowledge about the apparent-real and pretend-real distinctions. *Developmental Psychology, 23*, pp. 816-22.

Dement, W. C. (1974). *Some must watch while some must sleep* (pp. 24-26). San Francisco: W. H. Freeman.

Gergen, K. J. (1991). *The saturated self: Dilemmas of identity in contemporary life* (pp.61-63). New York: Basic Books.
Reference cited in excerpt
Quinone, R. (1985). *Mapping literary modernism*. Princeton, NJ: Princeton University Press.

Healy, J. M. (1990). *Endangered minds: Why our children don't think* (pp. 120-122). New York: Simon & Schuster.
Reference cited in excerpt
Sassy: Like, you know, for kids. (1988, September 18). *The New York Times*.

James, W. (1948). *Psychology* (pp.179-181). Cleveland, OH: World Publishing.

Jenkins, M. D. (1971). The upper limits of ability among American Negroes. In R. C. Wilcox, *The psychological consequences of being a black American: A sourcebook of research by Black Americans* (pp. 102-106). New York: Wiley. (Original work published 1948)

Kagan, J. (1971). *Understanding children: Behavior, motives, and thought* (pp. 101-102). New York: Harcourt Brace Jovanovich.

Krueger, M. W. (1991). *Artificial reality II* (2nd ed.) (pp. 124-126). Reading, MA: Addison-Wesley.

Latané, B., & Darley, J. M. (1970). *The unresponsive bystander: Why doesn't he help?* (pp.24-26). New York: Appleton-Century-Crofts.

Levine, J. A. (1976). *Who will raise the children? New options for fathers (and mothers)* (pp. 130-132). Philadelphia: Lippincott.

Loftus, E., & Ketcham, K. (1991). *Witness for the defense: The accused, the eyewitness, and the expert who puts memory on trial* (pp. 20-22). New York: St. Martin's Press.

Lorenz, K. Z. (1952). *King Solomon's ring* (pp. 76-79). New York: Harper & Row.

BIBLIOGRAPHY, *continued*

McAndrews, L. (1990). *My father forgets* (pp. 68-71). Maple City, MI: Northern Publishing.

Ornstein, R. (1993). *The roots of the self: Unraveling the mystery of who we are* (pp. 1-3). San Francisco: Harper San Francisco.

Reynolds, D. K. (1980). *The quiet therapies: Japanese pathways to personal growth* (pp. 21-22). Honolulu: The University Press of Hawaii.
Reference cited in excerpt
Ohara, K., & Reynolds, D. (n.d.) *Morita psychotherapy: Characteristics of a Japanese treatment for neurosis*. Unpublished manuscript.

Rogoff, B. (1990). *Apprenticeship in thinking: Cognitive development in social context* (pp. 122-124). New York: Oxford University Press.
References cited in excerpt
Morelli, G. A., Fitz, D., Oppenheim, D., Nash, A., Nakagawa, M., & Rogoff, B. (1988, November). *Social relations in infants' sleeping arrangements*. Paper presented at the meeting of the American Anthropological Association, Phoenix, AZ.
Ochs, E., & Schieffelin, B. B. (1984). Language acquisition and socialization: Three developmental stories and their implications. In R. Schweder & R. LeVine (Eds.), *Culture and its acquisition*. Chicago: University of Chicago Press.
Rogoff, B. (1981a). Adults and peers as agents of socialization: A Highland Guatemalan profile. *Ethos, 9*, pp. 18-36.
Ward, M. C. (1971). *Them children: A study in language learning*. New York: Holt, Rinehart and Winston.
Whiting, J.W.M. (1981). Environmental constraints on infant care practices. In R. H. Munroe, R. L. Munroe, & B. B. Whiting (Eds.), *Handbook of cross-cultural human development*. New York: Garland.

Styron, W. (1990). *Darkness visible: A memoir of madness* (pp. 45-46, 58-59, 75-77). New York: Random House.

Voydanoff, P. (1993). Work and family relationships. In T. H. Brubaker (Ed.), *Family relations: Challenges for the future* (pp. 100-102). Newbury Park, CA: Sage.
References cited in excerpt
Aldous, J. (1978). *Family careers: Developmental change in families*. New York: Wiley.
Bailyn, L., & Schein, E. (1976). *Life/career considerations as indicators of quality of employment: Measuring work quality for social reporting*. Newbury Park, CA: Sage.
Brody, E. M. (1985). Parent care as normative family stress. *The Gerontologist, 25*, pp. 19-29.
Cohen, J. (1979). Male roles in mid-life. *Family Coordinator, 28*, pp. 465-471.

Hall, F. S., & Hall, D. T. (1979). *The two-career couple*. Reading, MA: Addison-Wesley.
Harry, J. (1976). Evolving sources of happiness for men over the life cycle: A structural analysis. *Journal of Marriage and the Family, 38*, pp. 289-296.
Hill, R. (1964). Methodological issues in family development research. *Family Process, 3*, pp. 186-206.
Kelly, R. F., & Voydanoff, P. (1985). Work/family role strain among employed parents. *Family Relations, 34*, pp. 367-374.
Pleck, J. H. (1977, May). *Developmental stages in men's lives: How do they differ from women's?* Paper presented at the Conference on Resocialization of Sex Roles: Challenge for the 1970s, Hartland, MI.
Voydanoff, P., & Kelly, R. F. (1984). Determinants of work-related family problems among employed parents. *Journal of Marriage and the Family, 46*, pp. 881-892.
Wilensky, H. (1961). Orderly careers and social participation. *American Sociological Review, 26*, pp. 521-539.
Voydanoff, P. (1987). *Work and family life*. Newbury Park, CA: Sage.

Yeo, J. (1996, June). Readers write: Faces. *The Sun: A Magazine of Ideas*, p. 36.

CHAPTER 1

WHAT IS PSYCHOLOGY?

The preeminent professional organization for psychologists is the American Psychological Association (APA). Since its founding by G. Stanley Hall in 1892, the APA has set rules of conduct for the various aspects of psychological work. Acceptance of membership in the APA commits a person to adhere to the APA Ethics Code and to the rules and procedures that have been established to implement it. The excerpt that follows is the section regarding ethics in research from the 2003 edition of *Ethical Principles of Psychologists and Code of Conduct*.

8.01   Institutional Approval

When institutional approval is required, psychologists provide accurate information about their research proposals and obtain approval prior to conducting the research. They conduct the research in accordance with the approved research protocol.

8.02   Informed Consent to Research

(a) When obtaining informed consent as required in Standard 3.10, Informed Consent, psychologists inform participants about (1) the purpose of the research, expected duration, and procedures; (2) their right to decline to participate and to withdraw from the research once participation has begun; (3) the foreseeable consequences of declining or withdrawing; (4) reasonably foreseeable factors that may be expected to influence their willingness to participate such as potential risks, discomfort, or adverse effects; (5) any prospective research benefits; (6) limits of confidentiality; (7) incentives for participation; and (8) whom to contact for questions about the research and research participants' rights. They provide opportunity for the prospective participants to ask questions and receive answers.

(b) Psychologists conducting intervention research involving the use of experimental treatments clarify to participants at the outset of the research (1) the experimental nature of the treatment; (2) the services that will or will not be available to the control group(s) if appropriate; (3) the means by which assignment to treatment and control groups will be made; (4) available treatment alternatives if an individual does not wish to participate in the research or wishes to withdraw once a study has begun; and (5) compensation for or monetary costs of participating including, if appropriate, whether reimbursement from the participant or a third-party payor will be sought.

8.03   Informed Consent for Recording Voices and Images in Research

Psychologists obtain informed consent from research participants prior to recording their voices or images for data collection unless (1) the research consists solely of naturalistic observations in public places, and it is not anticipated that the recording will be used in a manner that could cause personal identification or harm, or (2) the research design includes deception, and consent for the use of the recording is obtained during debriefing.

8.04   Client/Patient, Student, and Subordinate Research Participants

(a) When psychologists conduct research with clients/patients, students, or subordinates as participants, psychologists take steps to protect the prospective participants from adverse consequences of declining or withdrawing from participation.

(b) When research participation is a course requirement or an opportunity for extra credit, the prospective participant is given the choice of equitable alternative activities.

8.05 Dispensing With Informed Consent for Research

Psychologists may dispense with informed consent only (1) where research would not reasonably be assumed to create distress or harm and involves (a) the study of normal educational practices, curricula, or classroom management methods conducted in educational settings; (b) only anonymous not place participants at risk of criminal or civil liability or damage their financial standing, employability, or reputation, and confidentiality is protected; or (c) the study of factors related to job or organization effectiveness conducted in organizational settings for which there is no risk to participants' employability, and confidentiality is protected or (2) where otherwise permitted by law or federal or institutional regulations.

8.06 Offering Inducements for Research Participation

(a) Psychologists make reasonable efforts to avoid offering excessive or inappropriate financial or other inducements for research participation when such inducements are likely to coerce participation.

(b) When offering professional services as an inducement for research participation, psychologists clarify the nature of the services, as well as the risks, obligations, and limitations.

8.07 Deception in Research

(a) Psychologists do not conduct a study involving deception unless they have determined that the use of deceptive techniques is justified by the study's significant prospective scientific, educational, or applied value and that effective nondeceptive alternative procedures are not feasible.

(b) Psychologists do not deceive prospective participants about research that is reasonably expected to cause physical pain or severe emotional distress.

(c) Psychologists explain any deception that is an integral feature of the design and conduct of an experiment to participants as early as is feasible, preferably at the conclusion of their participation, but no later than at the conclusion of the data collection, and permit participants to withdraw their data.

QUESTIONS

1. What are the two situations in which a psychologist may dispense with informed consent?

2. According to the Ethics Code, should psychologists pay or offer other inducements to their research participants? Do you think participants should be paid? Why or why not?

3. What is one type of research in which psychologists should never deceive prospective participants?

CHAPTER

2 PSYCHOLOGICAL METHODS

Nobel Prize winner Konrad Lorenz (1903-1989), an Australian naturalist, was one of the founders of ethology—the study of animal behavior. Unlike psychologists at the time, who relied heavily on laboratory studies of animal behavior, Lorenz conducted his observations in the field. Today the practice of observing people and animals in their natural environment, which is referred to as *naturalistic observation,* is an established method of psychological research on behavior. In scientific research, the term *observing* means more than casual watching. Scientific observers of behavior look for minute signals that provide insight into the factors that cause or result from that behavior. The following excerpt from Lorenz's book *King Solomon's Ring* reveals how carefully and completely Lorenz observed his animal subjects.

Animals do not possess a language in the true sense of the word. In the higher vertebrates, as also in insects, particularly in the socially living species of both great groups, every individual has a certain number of innate movements and sounds for expressing feelings. It has also innate ways of reacting to these signals whenever it sees or hears them in a fellow-member of the species. The highly social species of birds such as the jackdaw or the greylag goose have a complicated code of such signals which are uttered and understood by every bird without any previous experience. The perfect coordination of social behavior which is brought about by these actions and reactions conveys to the human observer the impression that the birds are talking and understanding a language of their own. Of course, this purely innate signal code of an animal species differs fundamentally from human language, every word of which must be learned laboriously by the human child. Moreover, being a genetically fixed character of the species—just as much as any bodily character—this so-called language is, for every individual animal species, ubiquitous [present everywhere] in its distribution. Obvious though this fact may seem, it was, nevertheless, with something akin to naive surprise that I heard the jackdaws in northern Russia "talk" exactly the same, familiar "dialect" as my birds at home in Altenberg. The superficial similarity between these animal utterances and human languages diminishes further as it becomes gradually clear to the observer that the animal, in all these sounds and movements expressing its emotions, has in no way the conscious intention of influencing a fellow-member of its species. This is proved by the fact that even geese or jackdaws reared and kept singly make all these signals as soon as the corresponding mood overtakes them. Under these circumstances the automatic and even mechanical character of these signals becomes strikingly apparent and reveals them as entirely different from human words.

In human behavior, too, there are mimetic [imitative] signs which automatically transmit a certain mood and which escape one without or even contrary to one's intention of thereby influencing anybody else: the commonest example of this is yawning. Now the mimetic sign by which the yawning mood manifests itself is an easily perceived optical and acoustical stimulus whose effect is, therefore, not particularly surprising. But, in general, such crude and patent signals are not always necessary in order to transmit a mood. On the contrary, it is characteristic of this particular effect that it is often brought about by diminutive sign stimuli which are hardly perceptible by conscious observation. The mysterious apparatus for transmitting and receiving the sign stimuli which convey moods is age-old, far older than mankind itself. In our own case, it has doubtless degenerated as our word-language developed. Man has no need of minute intention-displaying movements to announce his momentary mood: he can say it in words. But jackdaws or dogs are obliged to "read in each other's eyes" what they are about to do in the next moment. For this reason, in higher and social animals, the transmitting, as well as the receiving, apparatus of "mood-convection" is much better developed and more highly specialized than in us humans. All expressions of animal emotions, for instance, the "Kia" and "Kiaw" note of the jackdaw, are therefore not comparable to our spoken language, but only to those expressions such as yawning, wrinkling the brow and smiling, which are expressed unconsciously as innate actions and also understood by a corresponding inborn mechanism. The "words" of the various animal "languages" are merely interjections.

Though man may also have numerous gradations of unconscious mimicry, no George Robey or Emil Jannings [professional actors] would be able, in this sense, to convey, by mere miming, as the greylag goose can, whether he was going to walk or fly, or to indicate whether he wanted to go home or to venture further afield, as a jackdaw can do quite easily. Just as the transmitting apparatus of animals is considerably more efficient than that of man, so also is their receiving apparatus, This is not only capable of distinguishing a large number of signals, but, to preserve the above simile, it responds to much slighter transmissions than does our own. It is incredible, what minimal signs, completely imperceptible to man, animals will receive and interpret rightly. Should one member of a jackdaw flock that is seeking for food on the ground, fly upwards merely to seat itself on the nearest apple-tree and preen its feathers, then none of the others will cast so much as a glance in its direction; but, if the bird takes to wing with intent to cover a longer distance, then it will be joined, according to its authority as a member of the flock, by its spouse or also a larger group of jackdaws, in spite of the fact that it did not emit a single "Kia."

QUESTIONS

1. According to Lorenz, what type of communication preceded word-language in humans? Do you think he would have come to the same conclusion if he had observed animals only in the laboratory?

2. If you have ever been able to predict an animal's intended behavior by observing hardly perceptible signs, describe the incident.

3. Do you think that humans can send or receive nearly imperceptible signals of planned behavior to or from particular people? Why or why not?

From *King Solomon's Ring* by Konrad Lorenz. Copyright © 1952 by Harper & Row. Published by Methuen & Company. Reprinted by permission of *Routledge*.

BIOLOGY AND BEHAVIOR

Alzheimer's disease is a degenerative brain disease that affects about 10 percent of people over the age of 65. As the brain deteriorates from Alzheimer's, behavior is affected. Eventually, the person may lose all ability to reason. Witnessing these changes in behavior is usually very difficult for the family of the person with Alzheimer's disease. The following excerpt is from the book *My Father Forgets*. In it, author Lynn McAndrews chronicles the changes she and her family observed firsthand in her father, John Dechow, as the disease took hold of him. In this part of the book, Mr. Dechow has just been brought to a hospital, called Center One, for observation, tests, and diagnosis.

Dad's demeanor for the two weeks in Center One was jovial and generally docile. He wandered unwittingly into other patients' rooms and became lost easily. Once he strayed from the floor and was found in another section of the hospital. He spit some of his medications into the toilet and left the water running for no reason. The nurses watched him closely.

He mentioned to one nurse that he had run out of the house the day before because someone was trying to shoot him. In the last few months he had expressed fear that my mother would "run around" with another man. The paranoia surrounding this subject was now becoming paramount in his mind. He mentioned the subject repeatedly to the doctor and nurses and told them that this man was taking his belongings while he was in the hospital. The convolutions of his now demented mind seemed to become more and more difficult to unravel.

One morning he called my mother at home. Painfully, she reassured him she wasn't running around on him. He continued telling the nurse about her going places and having a married man over all the time. Briefly he mentioned that the fellow's wife was his own daughter, but the family connection was becoming irrelevant. All that mattered was that his wife was hanging around with another man.

There were times when he thought he was home. When walking in the hallway, he had his rubber boots and felt liners on. When asked whether these weren't too hot for indoor attire, he replied, "I might have to go to the garage, and I'll get my feet wet." One time he said he was looking for tools under the bed. Other times he would be looking for his father, who had been dead for more than 35 years.

He searched for my mother in the hallway and in other patients' rooms. He walked in and said, "How is my wife?" When he continually had trouble finding his room, the staff put a sign on his door with the word "JOHN" in foot-high letters. Sometimes the sign helped.

Despite his troubled fantasies about Mother and his frustration at not being able to remember names, he was jovial with the staff and appreciative of the care they gave him. When the psychiatrist finished talking to him for the day and started to leave the room, he followed her and said, "I'm not done yet. Listen to this one. I've got a good one for you," as if telling another joke. Sometimes she sat and listened to "one more," even though it made little sense.

One who listened well was my brother Paul. He came to see Dad a few days after admission. Paul remembers his trying to tell the events of the past few days—going to an unfamiliar house, being afraid the owner was going to come home, seeing another man in the house. The account didn't make much sense, but Paul understood some of it and could see the desperation behind it. Dad clearly knew Paul and found comfort in his ability to listen. Seeing a fresh face different from the characters he had been dealing with was welcome.

My father received a lot of attention on this ward, including attempts by the staff to play Yahtzee with him. He had always enjoyed this simple dice game, but now he couldn't even follow the instructions necessary for play. Yet one day my mother, Jim and I took him for a walk and ended up in the recreation room. There were a piano, some comfortable seats, and a Ping-Pong table. I suggested playing the piano and singing, but he made a gesture that he wanted to play Ping-Pong, an activity he rarely engaged in. The paddles were on the table, but I had to obtain the balls from the desk. I went quickly for fear his enthusiasm would wane.

He played Ping-Pong as well as he had done badly at Yahtzee. It was as if his motor skills would outlast his mental capacity for remembering number games. This man, who had rarely played Ping-Pong in his life, deftly hit the ball with spin and finesse. I played and watched at the same time, amazed at the step back in time we seemed to be taking. He laughed and even said a few things, and his otherwise self-conscious attitude temporarily disappeared. We were having pure unadulterated fun, which we rarely ever had together. The incident is etched in my memory, especially his smile. The smile was all there was that day. For a brief moment all was well. A few times he walked to another part of the room, but for the most part he focused on the playing. Suddenly, by leaving us and wandering into the hallway, he stopped the activity as quickly as he had started. He had played for 20 to 30 minutes, and now it was time to leave.

A few days later he had a consultation with a neurologist. Upon entering my father's room, the doctor noted that he was lying fully clothed in the bed and needed almost a minute to disentangle himself from the bedspread. He told the doctor his name was "John Dechow," but said his middle name was "Viola." His identification with my mother was complete. He was able to comply with some simple commands, but when asked to point to his left knee, he indicated instead the little finger on his left hand. When asked what a triangle is, he said, "It shows an intelligent person which way to go."

Later, the psychiatrist called us in to a comfortable meeting room to discuss my father's condition. She had consulted with the neurologist, who said in his report that the likelihood of Alzheimer's disease should be considered. She related that the diagnosis could not be determined definitely until after death, but that all signs pointed to Alzheimer's.

QUESTIONS

1. From the excerpt, which kind of skills seemed to be least affected by the deterioration of Mr. Dechow's brain at this point?

2. What trait did Mr. Dechow seem to appreciate in those who cared for him?

3. Why do you think is it so difficult for family members to witness the behavior changes brought on by Alzheimer's disease?

From *My Father Forgets* by Lynn McAndrews. Copyright © 1990 by Lynn McAndrews. Reprinted by permission of the author.

CHAPTER

4

SENSATION AND PERCEPTION

Scientists such as Myron Krueger, who carry out experiments in artificial reality, have made many discoveries about how people perceive reality. Many people consider Krueger to be the "father" of artificial reality, which he describes as follows: "An artificial reality perceives a participant's action in terms of the body's relationship to a graphic world and generates responses that maintain the illusion that his actions are taking place within that world." A common form of artificial reality today is movie rides. All forms of artificial-reality experiences reveal much about the way people process data and perceive their environment—both real and artificial.

Krueger discusses these issues in his book *Artificial Reality II*. In the excerpt that follows, he shares a personal experience that is evidence that, although our perceptions are formed by the sensory impulses that our sense organs transmit to our brain, the brain apparently does not treat the data from all organs equally. To make an artificial environment effective, manipulation of the senses is necessary.

Introduction

An artificial reality must dominate the participant's senses with synthetic stimuli that define a context for an experience that the person will accept as real, even if the world portrayed is not. All of the senses are candidates for illusory input. However, in terms of their importance for creating artificial realities, sight and hearing almost certainly dominate, followed by touch, with smell and taste of lesser significance. Fortunately, there has been a revolution in our ability to produce real-time graphics and computer-controlled sound. These developments, together with the appearance of inexpensive flat panel displays, have made possible the artificial realities that we see today.

Visual Expectations

The most important and best understood sense is vision, which more than any other provides us with our sense of place. When visual cues conflict with data received by the other senses, they usually dominate. This dominance results from expectations based on eons of evolution and a lifetime of experience with physical reality. The following example is taken from personal experience and illustrates the importance of these expectations.

Mystery Ride

Many years ago on the Boardwalk at Ocean City, New Jersey, there was a concession called the Mystery Ride. A group of about ten people entered a very ordinary room, complete with pictures on the walls, a light fixture hanging from the ceiling, and a rug on the floor. We were seated on two benches suspended by heavy beams from either end of the room. When the ride began, it seemed we were being turned upside down. This was alarming as there were no physical restraints to keep us on our benches. After a panicky moment, I reasoned that it was the room that was turning around us, while we remained stationary. Unfortunately, this intelligence was not at all reassuring, for years of experience tell us that ceilings are up and floors are down, and when we find our head by the floor and our feet by the ceiling, we assume that we are upside down.

► **CHAPTER 4,** *continued*

I closed my eyes to rely on my vestibular sense. The semicircular canals in my inner ear, which are responsible for my sense of balance and had served to make me seasick in the past, were now being asked to offer evidence in support of intellect in its case against untrustworthy vision. Unfortunately, the authority of the visual interpretation made the interior sense unreadable. Although I was familiar with the psychological literature describing visual illusions, I had never guessed how dramatically vision was able to tyrannize the other senses, and to overrule reason as well.

This illusion suggests that there are conventions established by our visual experience that can be exploited for use in an environmental display. More than the other senses, vision defines reality or unreality. We can become disoriented and even unbalanced if the relationships anticipated by our sense of sight are altered. Consider a gymnast standing on a balance beam while wearing reality goggles. It would almost certainly be impossible for her to keep her balance if the computer graphic world was tilted with respect to the real one.

QUESTIONS

1. What sense does Krueger think is the most dominant? Do you agree? Why or why not?

2. What experience have you had where your vision or hearing, at least momentarily, overruled reason?

3. Do you think the perceptions that people have while in an artificial-reality environment are real? Why or why not?

5 CONSCIOUSNESS

When studying or discussing sleep, scientists usually divide the topic of sleep into stages. The stage of sleep in which we dream is referred to as rapid-eye-movement sleep, or REM sleep. The person who coined this term is William C. Dement, whose expertise in the study of sleep is acclaimed worldwide. Although long associated with the Stanford University Sleep Disorders Clinic and Laboratories in Stanford, California, the phenomenon of REM sleep was discovered at the University of Chicago, in Chicago, Illinois. In the following excerpt from his book *Some Must Watch While Some Must Sleep,* Dement recounts the discovery of REM sleep during his student days in 1952.

The Discovery of REM Sleep

Every day every human being—every mammal, in fact—experiences two kinds of sleep that alternate rhythmically throughout the entire sleep period. These two kinds of sleep are as different from each other as sleep is from wakefulness. If there is a cat or a dog in your household, chances are you have observed the two states of sleep many times. At one moment the sleeping animal seems to be lifeless except for its regular breathing. Then the breathing becomes irregular, paws and whiskers begin to twitch, lips and tongue begin to move—and someone says, "Oh, look at Rover! He's *dreaming!*"

The discovery of the two kinds of sleep occurred almost accidentally at the University of Chicago. In 1952, Dr. Kleitman became interested in the slow rolling eye movements that accompany sleep onset and decided to look for these eye movements throughout the night to determine whether they were related to the depth or quality of sleep. Kleitman gave the assignment of watching eye movements to one of his graduate students in the department of physiology, Eugene Aserinsky.

The young student soon noticed an entirely new kind of eye movement. At certain times during the night, the eyes began to dart about furiously beneath the closed lids. These unexpected episodes were startlingly different from the familiar slow, pendular movements that were the original object of the study.

Over the years, many people have asked me, "How can you see the eye moving when the lids are closed?" As a matter of fact, it is very easy to see eye movements when the eyes are closed. Have someone do it and see for yourself. However, Aserinsky was using the polygraph to monitor the subject, and the eye movements were actually discovered on the chart paper. It was not until he directly observed these movements in sleeping subjects that he could believe the spectacular inked out deviations. It would be difficult today to understand how skeptical we were. These eye movements, which had all the attributes of waking eye movements, had absolutely no business appearing in sleep. In those days, sleep was conceived of as a state of neural depression or inhibition— quiescence, rest. It was definitely not a condition in which the brain could be generating highly coordinated eye movements that were, in many instances, faster and sharper than the subject could execute while awake.

I have always felt that this was *the* breakthrough—the discovery that changed the course of sleep research from a relatively pedestrian inquiry into an intensely exciting endeavor pursued with great determination in laboratories and clinics all over the world. And there is nothing more exciting to a researcher than findings that are totally different from what he had expected.

Of course, the change in all our concepts of sleep didn't occur overnight. Having joined the research effort at this point as a sophomore medical student under Kleitman, I began to record the electroencephalograph and other physiological variables, along with eye movement activity. Since I didn't know what to expect, I kept my eyes glued to the moving chart paper all night long. After many nights, certain definite relationships were discernible in the enormous amounts of data. Rapid eye movements were always accompanied by very distinctive brain wave patterns, a change in breathing, and other striking departures from the normal, quiet sleep pattern. In addition, what we now call the basic ninety-minute sleep pattern began to emerge from the night-to-night variability.

As more and more physiological changes were discovered and described, we realized that sleep was not a quiet resting state that continued without variance as long as the subject was fortunate enough to remain asleep. No. For the first time we realized what has probably been true of man's sleep since he crawled out of the primordial slime. Man has *two* kinds of sleep. His nocturnal solitude contains two entirely different phenomena.

REM and NREM Sleep

I coined the term "REM" (for rapid-eye-movement) sleep to define the phenomenon my colleagues and I had observed. The other kind of sleep eventually acquired the name "NREM" (pronounced non-REM) sleep.

Most of the changes typically associated with falling asleep are the consequence of reclining and relaxing. Cardiac and respiratory rates will decrease, body temperature will fall, blood pressure will decline, and metabolic activity will drop. If we continue to lie still and relax, we may fall asleep without the occurrence of any further changes.

The NREM state is often called "quiet sleep" because of the slow, regular breathing, the general absence of body movement, and the slow, regular brain activity shown in the EEG. It is important to remember that the body is not paralyzed during NREM sleep; it *can* move, but it *does not* move because the brain doesn't order it to move. The sleeper has lost contact with his environment. There is a shutdown of perception because the five senses are no longer gathering information and communicating stimuli to the brain. When gross body movements (such as rolling over) occur during NREM, the EEG suggests a transient intrusion of wakefulness—yet the individual may not be responsive at the time, nor recall having moved if subsequently awakened. In one respect the term "quiet sleep" is a misnomer: it is during NREM sleep that snoring occurs.

QUESTIONS

1. What does Dement consider the breakthrough discovery that elevated sleep research in the science community?

2. Who do you think should be credited with the discovery of REM sleep? Why?

3. Would you expect Dement to feel discouraged if the results of an experiment did not prove his hypothesis? Why or why not?

From *Some Must Watch While Some Must Sleep* by **William C. Dement.** Copyright © 1974 by **William C. Dement.** Used by permission of **W. H. Freeman and Company.**

CHAPTER 6

LEARNING

Many psychologists consider the cognitive development of children to be an apprenticeship. It other words, children learn by guided participation in social activities that introduce and refine their understanding of and skill in using the tools and the language of the culture. This is also how children learn to follow the ways of dealing with life that are common to the culture. Research has shown that the way adults interact with children varies from culture to culture. The excerpt that follows—taken from Barbara Rogoff's book *Apprenticeship in Thinking: Cognitive Development in Social Context*—compares the adult/child learning status in several cultures in which she has conducted research about the ways that children learn.

In the Mayan community in which I have worked, children seldom interact with adults as conversational partners, but engage with adults during their participation in adult activities, taught by demonstration (which includes talk) in context. Children are freed from direct supervision by adults by age 3 or 4 and then move around town with a multi-age group of children, amusing themselves by observing ongoing events and imitating their elders in play. Infants were always with adults and interacted with them (not necessarily in conversation) on 50% of the daytime occasions I observed. But by ages 3 to 4, children were less often with adults and interacted with them on fewer than 10% of the occasions, with further drops in adult companionship from age 5 throughout childhood (Rogoff, 1981a). Children participated in household work beginning by age 5, taking responsibility for sweeping, some food preparation, and child care.

When older children did interact with adults, it was in the context of participation in adult work. Adults were as likely as or more likely than peers to be interacting with 9-year-olds when the children were engaged in household or agricultural work, but were almost never involved with them when children were playing. Play was a domain for peer interaction, not adult companionship. Even in play, though, the children emulated adult roles: 66% of their play (excluding sports) involved imitation of adult roles. But of the 1,708 observations of 9-year-olds out of school, native observers identified only 6 occasions as teaching situations.

Ochs and Schieffelin (1984) suggest that there may be two cultural patterns of speech between young children and their caregivers. In cultures that adapt situations to children (as in middle-class U.S. families), caregivers simplify their talk, negotiate meaning with children, cooperate with them in building propositions, and respond to their verbal and nonverbal initiations. In cultures that adapt children to the normal situations of the society (as in Kaluli New Guinea and Samoan families), caregivers model unsimplified utterances for children to repeat to a third party, direct them to notice others, and build interaction around circumstances to which the caregivers wish the children to respond. . . .

In all these patterns, the child participates in activities of the society, but the patterns vary in terms of the child's or the caregiver's responsibility to adapt in the process of learning or teaching the more mature forms of speech and action.

The adaptation of caregivers to children may be necessary in societies that segregate children from adult activities, thus requiring them to practice skills or learn information outside the mature context of use (Rogoff, 1981a). In the U.S. middle class, many school-age children do not even know what their parents' occupations are, much less how their parents carry out adult work and adult interaction. They are segregated from the occupational and recreational world of adults, and learn about skills they may eventually need in order to participate in their society as adults in a separate context specialized for the purpose—school. (In an age-segregated society, such lessons in development continue in adulthood, with classes in childbirth, handling toddlers, and adjusting to various phases of adulthood, since individuals face new phases of development without much opportunity to observe others at different phases and thereby to pick up examples and ideas of the next step directly.)

At home, young children in an age-segregated community such as the U.S. middle class seldom have much chance to participate in the functioning of the household, and may be segregated from human company by the provision of separate bedrooms, security *objects,* and attractive toys. Middle-class infants are in the unusual situation (speaking in worldwide terms) of being entirely alone for as much as 10 hours of a 24-hour day, managing as best they can to handle their hunger or thirst with a bottle and their need for comforting with a pacifier or blanky or teddy, and working, as Margaret Mead put it, to establish their independence in the transitions to sleep and waking in the night and at naptime (Morelli, et al., 1988; Ward, 1971; Whiting, 1981). During waking hours, their involvement with adults is focused on entertaining themselves while their parents get some work done or on parental interaction that is focused at the children's level, with adjustment of speech and activities to their skill and understanding.

In societies in which children are integrated in adult activities, the children are ensured a role in the action, at least as close observers. Children are present at most events of interest in the community, from work to recreation to church. They are able to observe and eavesdrop on the ongoing processes of life and death, work and play, that are important in their community. As infants, they are often carried wherever their mothers or older siblings go, and as young children, they may do errands and roam the town in their free time, watching whatever is going on. As nonparticipants in ordinary adult conversation, they may be free to eavesdrop on important adult activities from which nonparticipant adults may be excluded.

QUESTIONS

1. What are the two cultural patterns of speech between young children and their caregivers that researchers have identified?
2. Which of the above patterns is common in your culture? What examples can you think of that are evidence of this?
3. When you interact with young children, do you alter your vocabulary or sentence structure? Why or why not?

Note: Information for cited references appears in Bibliography. (See page 3.)

From *Apprenticeship in Thinking* by Barbara Rogoff. Copyright © 1991 by Barbara Rogoff. Reprinted by permission of *Oxford University Press, Inc.*

CHAPTER

7

MEMORY

To help juries evaluate eyewitness testimony, expert witnesses are often called to testify. Dr. Elizabeth Loftus, a psychologist and expert in memory and the fallibility of eyewitness testimony, is often called as an expert trial witness. In the following excerpt from the book *Witness for the Defense*, which she wrote with Katherine Ketcham, Loftus explains the weight that eyewitness testimony lends to a case and why eyewitnesses' recollections of what they "know" they saw may be wrong. The excerpt begins by comparing the mind to a filing cabinet, where memories are stored in mental "drawers" somewhere in the brain.

The "drawers" holding our memories are obviously extremely densely packed. They are also constantly being emptied out, and then stuffed back into place. Like curious, playful children searching through drawers for a blouse or pair of pants, our brains seem to enjoy ransacking the memory drawers, tossing the facts about, and then stuffing everything back in, oblivious to order or importance. As new bits and pieces of information are added into long-term memory, the old memories are removed, replaced, crumpled up, or shoved into corners. Little details are added, confusing or extraneous elements are deleted, and a coherent construction of the facts is gradually created that may bear little resemblance to the original event.

Memories don't just fade, as the old saying would have us believe; they also grow. What fades is the initial perception, the actual experience of the events. But every time we recall an event, we must reconstruct the memory, and with each recollection the memory may be changed—colored by succeeding events, other people's recollections or suggestions, increased understanding, or a new context.

Truth and reality, when seen through the filter of our memories, are not objective facts but subjective, interpretative realities. We interpret the past, correcting ourselves, adding bits and pieces, deleting uncomplementary or disturbing recollections, sweeping, dusting, tidying things up. Thus our representation of the past takes on a living, shifting reality; it is not fixed and immutable, not a place way back there that is preserved in stone, but a living thing that changes shape, expands, shrinks, and expands again, an amoebalike creature with powers to make us laugh, and cry, and clench our fists. Enormous powers—powers even to make us believe in something that never happened.

Are we aware of our mind's distortions of our past experiences? In most cases, the answer is no. As time goes by and the memories gradually change, we become convinced that we saw or said or did what we remember. We perceive the blending of fact and fiction that constitutes a memory as completely and utterly truthful. We are innocent victims of our mind's manipulations.

A pointing finger of blame has a powerful hold on even the most intelligent of juries. Several years ago I conducted an experiment in which subjects acted as jurors in a criminal case. First they heard a description of a robbery-murder, then a prosecution argument for the defense. In one version of the experiment, the prosecutor presented only circumstantial evidence; faced with this evidence, only 18 percent of the "jurors" found the "defendant" guilty. In a second version, the prosecutor pled the exact case with one difference: There was testimony from a single eyewitness—a clerk who identified the defendant as the robber. Now 72 percent of the jurors found the defendant guilty.

The danger of eyewitness testimony is clear: Anyone in the world can be convicted of a crime he or she did not commit, or deprived of an award that is due, based solely on the evidence of a witness who convinces a jury that his memory about what he saw is correct. Why is eyewitness testimony so powerful and convincing? Because people in general and jurors in particular believe that our memories stamp the facts of our experiences on a permanent, nonerasable tape, like a computer disk or videotape that is write-protected. For the most part, of course, our memories serve us reasonably well. But how often is precise memory demanded of us? When a friend describes a vacation, we don't ask, "Are you sure your hotel room had two chairs, not three?" After we watch a movie, our companion wouldn't normally grill us with questions like "Was Gene Hackman's hair wavy, or was it curly?" or "Did the woman in the bar wear red or pink lipstick?" If we make a mistake, it usually goes unnoticed and uncorrected—does it really matter if there were two chairs or three, or if the actor's hair was wavy or curly? Belief in an accurate memory is confirmed by default.

But precise memory suddenly becomes crucial in the event of a crime or an accident. Small details assume enormous importance. Did the assailant have a mustache, or was he clean shaven? Was he five eight or five eleven? Was the traffic light red, or was it green? How fast was the Cadillac going when it went through the red light—or was it yellow?—and smashed into the Volkswagen? Did the car cross the center line, or did it stay on its own side? Civil and criminal cases often rest on such subtle, seemingly trivial details, and these details are often hard to obtain.

In July 1977, *Flying* magazine reported the fatal crash of a small plane that killed all eight people aboard and one person who was on the ground. Sixty eyewitnesses were interviewed, and two eyewitnesses who had actually seen the airplane just before impact testified at a hearing to investigate the accident. The plane, one of the eyewitnesses explained, "was heading right toward the ground—straight down." This witness apparently did not know that several photographs clearly showed that the airplane hit flat and at a low-enough angle to skid for almost one thousand feet.

To be mistaken about details is not the result of a bad memory but of the normal functioning of human memory. When we want to remember something, we don't simply pluck a whole memory intact from a "memory store." The memory is actually constructed from stored and available bits of information; we unconsciously fill in any gaps in the information with inferences. When all the fragments are integrated into a whole that makes sense, they form what we call a memory.

QUESTIONS

1. According to the excerpt, are people aware of their mind's distortions of events?

2. Why is eyewitness testimony convincing?

3. Is a filing cabinet an accurate analogy for the human mind? Why or why not?

CHAPTER

8 THINKING AND LANGUAGE

In his book *Understanding Children,* Harvard psychologist Jerome Kagan examines how children think. In the following excerpt, Kagan provides an overview of how children solve problems.

The world of experience, like the printed page, is a puzzle that the child has to assemble in a way that makes sense to him. In order to solve the puzzle he must have the basic pieces, which are the cognitive structures. . . . He also needs to know how to put the pieces together. This function is described by the cognitive processes, to which we now turn our attention.

Cognitive processes—or more simply, thought—can be divided into two major types. In *undirected thought,* the mind is free of the burden of solving any problem and can wander in a variety of directions, skipping abruptly from idea to idea. Daydreams and the easy flow of ideas that occur when one is watching snow fall or upon waking in the morning are the best examples of undirected thought. It is difficult to study this important phenomenon because psychologists do not know how to probe the private nature of undirected thought without seriously disturbing it. If you ask a person to report his free associations— the thoughts that happen to be running through his mind—the question abruptly changes the fluid nature of his thinking, and what was undirected suddenly becomes directed.

The child who is asked a question has a problem to solve. As a result, he automatically attempts to organize a logical, coherent, and socially acceptable report of his thoughts. The request to report what he is thinking changes the nature of his thoughts and his subsequent reply will not contain the disorder or lack of logic that is often characteristic of undirected cognition. Thus *directed thought* involves all the cognitive processes that come into play when the child attempts to solve a problem, whether it is a problem he had set for himself or one that a teacher or parent has presented to him. When the child's thought is directed he is usually faced with a problem that he believes can be solved, and he knows when he has arrived at the solution.

The problem-solving process typically follows the following sequence. First, the child must comprehend the problem, whether it is presented orally or in written form. Next, he must hold the elements of the problem in his memory while he generates possible solutions. The child must then evaluate his understanding of the problem and the adequacy of his hypotheses. Finally, he must choose the best hypothesis and implement it. Under special circumstances, the child must also report the answer to someone. Thus the major processes in problem-solving are comprehension, memory, generation of ideas, evaluation of ideas, implementation, and occasionally public report. . . .

It is helpful to keep in mind . . . the general changes that occur over the period three through twelve years of age. The child's supply of schemata, images, symbols, concepts, and rules becomes richer and undergoes continual reorganization as a function of experience. The child becomes concerned with the degree of accord between his ideas and those of others, and he becomes more anxious about making mistakes. In addition, his ability to remember new facts and to recall old ones improves dramatically. Perhaps most important, his conception of problems and the rules he activates to solve them gradually approach those of the adult.

QUESTIONS

1. What two types of cognitive processes does Kagan describe?
2. Why, according to Kagan, is undirected thought difficult to measure?
3. What major problem-solving processes does Kagan list?

From *Understanding Children: Behavior, Motives, and Thought* by Jerome Kagan. Copyright © 1971 by Harcourt Brace Jovanovich, Inc. Reprinted by permission of the author.

CHAPTER

9

INTELLIGENCE

In 1905, French psychologist Alfred Binet published his first battery of tests intended to measure intelligence. Binet introduced the term *intelligence quotient,* or *IQ,* for a score representing an individual's intelligence as measured against a standard. In the countries that have administered tests to measure intelligence, IQ scores have soared dramatically since their introduction.

Explaining the cause of the sharp rise in IQ scores has captured the interest of many people. In April 1996, psychologist Ulrich Neisser of Emory University in Atlanta, Georgia, invited 16 researchers—including James R. Flynn, a political philosopher at the University of Otago in New Zealand, who stumbled upon the phenomenon, and psychologists Wendy Williams of Yale University and Patricia Greenfield of UCLA— to meet to discuss the issues that surround the consistently rising IQ scores. The following excerpt is from an article written about discussions at that meeting. The article is by journalist Sharon Begley and first appeared in the May 6, 1996, issue of *Newsweek.*

To some veterans of the "Bell Curve" debate, the sharp rise in IQ bolsters the argument that intelligence must be determined more by nurture than by nature. Nature, in the form of the prevalence of "smart" genes in a population, does not change at anything like the speed with which IQ has risen, goes the argument. "The gene pool cannot change so much, so fast," says John Boli of Emory University. But the Flynn effect might in fact be "consistent with either a high or a low heritability of intelligence," argues psychologist Stephen Ceci of Cornell University. He draws an analogy to height. Stature is strongly heritable: short parents have shorter children than tall parents do. Yet height, like IQ, has been rising for decades, not because tallness genes are suddenly more common but because of better nutrition. Similarly, intelligence may have a genetic basis yet still be subject to environmental influences. These influences would shape the form that intelligence takes in a particular society. They would also allow more children to attain their maximum intellectual potential—or keep them from doing so.

On a recent [1996] April weekend in Atlanta, psychologist Ulrich Neisser of Emory assembled 16 researchers to discuss these intriguing issues. Could rising living standards explain the IQ gain? Of the 20-odd-point rise, socioeconomic factors account for perhaps 5 points, Flynn calculates. Better schools? The greatest IQ gains have come on nonverbal intelligence tests—those that are heavy on mazes and puzzles. Yet these are the very tests that are designed to be free of such cultural influences as education. On tests of "acquired intelligence" (vocabulary or arithmetic or facts such as where turpentine comes from), which are expected to mirror acquired knowledge such as that from schooling, the gains are much smaller.

Might better nutrition and a more stimulating environment of museums and zoos, Legos and Transformers account for the IQ rise? Both can raise IQ scores, but only because they raise true intelligence by, say, giving the Legomaniac a better grasp of spatial relationships. And there is no evidence that real-world intelligence—an ability to learn faster or make creative leaps or do any of the other things that "intelligence" connotes—is rising at anything like the rate of IQ scores. (If it were, remember, the average American of 1918 couldn't have understood baseball.) Flynn calls this "the broken link" between IQ and intelligence.

At the Emory conference, Yale's Williams, an expert on the development of children's intelligence, pointed out that much of the IQ gain may simply reflect the greater familiarity that today's kids have with the sorts of questions posed on the tests. Taking her data from wherever she can find it, Williams has been collecting kids' cereal boxes and fast-food bags. Both are covered with mazes and puzzles remarkably similar to what IQ tests ask. "In the 1930s a kid may never have seen a maze before finding one on his IQ test," says Williams. "It seems clear that the tests are not for measuring innate, immutable intelligence, but a type of practiced learning and familiarity with the test questions."

But part of the IQ gain may reflect something far more meaningful, Williams suggested. Several studies indicate that a more permissive parenting style gives children a greater facility with language. "If the child is leading the parent, rather than always being directed, language skills develop faster," says Williams. "And language is closely linked to overall cognitive capacity. So while test-taking practice and a culture awash in mazes and puzzles would raise IQ scores without increasing intelligence in any meaningful way, parenting style may produce a true increase in intelligence and also in IQ."

Of all the explanations offered for the Flynn effect, Flynn himself is most taken with the idea that every generation comes of age in a world starkly different from their parents'. "Technological development has been going on in all the Flynn-effect countries," points out psychologist Patricia Greenfield of UCLA. And in some places formal schooling was greatly expanded during the same period. Whatever schools teach, they rely on the basic structure of test questions and answers. "The test question is the most basic convention on an intelligence test," says Greenfield. Children who have not had formal schooling would be unfamiliar with this format and therefore might do worse on standard IQ tests for reasons having nothing to do with their innate intelligence. More recently, Greenfield argues, wave upon wave of other cultural forces has lapped onto children's mental shores. Radio and TV drove up basic vocabulary. Videogames like Tetris enhanced such abilities as assembling a puzzle, a common IQ-test question. Action-packed videogames typically demand navigation through a two-dimensional representation of a 3-D space; mental paper folding, a prominent feature of the Stanford-Binet IQ test, demands the same skill. The spread of these image-intense technologies, says Greenfield, could explain the "spurt [in IQ scores] in the U.S. between 1972 and 1989."

QUESTIONS

1. According to this article, would you expect children with no formal schooling to do well on a standard IQ test? Why or why not?
2. What strategies prepare a student for an IQ test?
3. Do you think IQ tests test intelligence? Why or why not?

CHAPTER

10

INFANCY AND CHILDHOOD

One interesting aspect of child development is the development of imagination. Make-believe, daydreaming, creating imaginary companions, and pretending are all common activities for children as their imaginations develop. A less common form of imaginative activity that some children exhibit is the spontaneous creation of an imaginary world. This world can become quite detailed and can grow in complexity over the years. Some children keep their worlds totally secret, others share them with a sibling or friend, and some discuss them openly with the entire family. David Cohen and Stephen A. MacKeith, in their book *The Development of Imagination: The Private Worlds of Childhood*, reveal recollections of people who crafted imaginary worlds during their childhood. The following excerpts from that book tell of the imaginary worlds of two children— Leonora and Dickie.

Excerpt 1

LEONORA—PLAYING ORPHANS

When Leonora was about 7 or 8, she and two of her friends started The Game, which they played for some years whenever they were able to get together. They brought it to an end only when, at the onset of adolescence, they began to feel self-conscious about it.

The Game's setting was an orphanage, "a boarding establishment run by a particularly vicious couple." Leonora thinks the wife may have been modeled on a "narrow-minded religious woman" who had had charge of her family during her mother's temporary absence. The orphanage setting may have been inspired by "the horrible tales of life in an RC [Roman Catholic] boarding school" told to one of the three girls by an Irish domestic help.

The three girls were inmates in the orphanage, the terrifying warden and his wife being the central imaginary characters. The Game was the inventing and acting-out of incidents in the life of the orphanage, but these incidents had to be plausible. The Game was frequently inter-rupted for an ongoing discussion of our actions, e.g., "No, you can't possibly do that, it wouldn't be possible in the circumstances." . . . Injustice was a strong concept in our Game. Why *should* people have to put up with certain treatments?

The Game, though exclusive to its three players (one girl dropped out, but was replaced by another), was not secret: if their parents knew about it, they just left them to get on with it, not interfering in any way.

Leonora thinks, in retrospect, that the satisfactions which it gave them were "to do with creating a difficult challenge to be overcome. Basically [we] all had pretty easy childhoods; we enjoyed ourselves, our parents were OK, but we enjoyed beating the 'them' in Our Game."

She describes herself as having been a dreamy and scatterbrained lit-tle girl whom outsiders may have thought over-serious; "but that's just the way I was/am." . . . She could read at 3 1/2, and from then on, she was an omnivorous reader [read everything available]. Looking back, she recalls fantasies in which she delivered "devastating punch-lines in recurring arguments," but she doesn't recall much self-doubt, nor feel-ing the need for withdrawal from the real world, though, she says, "by implication, that was what The Game did for me/us."

Many of the imagined incidents of The Game were acted out by the participants, a practice which is common among young "paracosmists" [people who create imaginary worlds]. The proceedings were frequently interrupted for discussions about how plausible they were.

No theory of the imagination is sufficiently comprehensive to explain why, as they get older, children worry about whether a fantasy is real enough. Is it boredom? Or do children become embarrassed because they start to judge what their imagination produces with what they have been taught to recognize as truly imaginative?

Excerpt 2

DICKIE

At 5 years old Dickie already had a private world which meant a great deal to him. His father undertook to put to the child our questions about it, and to write down his answers.

Q. How old were you when you first began to have any imaginary world? Is it your very own, or do you share it with someone?

A. I really have got a farm. I was about 2. I go there at night. I walk or fly my kite.

Q. Do you make up stories about what happens in it? And do you do anything else about it, for instance, draw maps or make models of it?

A. I don't make up stories about it; but I am going to make maps and models of it.

Q. It must be fun, or you wouldn't do it. Can you give us some idea of what *makes* it fun?

A. What makes it fun? Things like Halloween, when I stay up late and have a party, and the animals have a merry dance outside.

Q. What other sorts of things do you specially like doing? And what sort of things do you really hate?

A. Throwing pies in the cow's face. Fighting, and playing marbles. I've got a big motorbike. I hate having to get dressed.

His father added that, during a recent family holiday, Dickie's farm was being quite seriously discussed by a group of adults. Dickie was present; after a time he crept close to his father and whispered "Tell them it isn't a *real* farm." (Such clear differentiation between pretense and reality develops in children at a very early age. See Flavell et al. 1987.) Dickie claims that his private world dates back to the age of 2. Even when questioned, he was only 5. Structured imagination can start early.

QUESTIONS

1. The authors cannot explain why it is that as children get older they worry that their fantasy may not be real enough. Why do you think children become more concerned with reality as they mature?
2. What influence do you think computers might have on incidents of contemporary children creating imaginary worlds? Why?
3. Did you or do you know anyone who invented an imaginary world during childhood? If so, how did that world compare with those described here?

Note: Information for cited reference appears in Bibliography. (See page 2.)

CHAPTER 11

ADOLESCENCE

As students move toward the adolescent period of development, they are expected to refine their language, listening, and thinking skills. By high school, teachers expect that students will have reached levels of these skills that are adequate for the educational purposes and activities of secondary school. For many years, teacher's expectations were, in general, fulfilled. Currently, however, as students reach grades that traditionally require higher-level thinking and organizational skills, ability to comprehend difficult books, and increased amounts of writing, many students are exhibiting skill levels that do not measure up to what many teachers require. One explanation for this apparent lag in language-based skills is that technology and evolving values are keeping children and youth isolated within their own culture.

The overall question of declining skills was explored by educational psychologist Jane M. Healy in her book *Endangered Minds*. In the following excerpt from that book, Healy makes the point that the communication style of many adolescents is stuck in the "primitive" category of an earlier stage of development. In this sense, the term *primitive* means simply that the language is unelaborated and might be considered nonacademic.

Code-Switching: From "Teenage" to English

To think and express themselves clearly, reason and write well, and understand what middle and high schools expect them to read, children need to learn the codes of formal education. Yet, the communication style of many adolescents, even when they are trying to cope with academic language, is often in the "primitive" category. And because they seem to be less able to "code-switch," they are even more at odds with the adult world than teens of previous eras.

It is nothing new for teenagers to talk differently in English class than when hanging out in the cafeteria. The itchy autonomy of adolescence requires its own lexicon [vocabulary]. Yet, in order to adapt to school demands, students must be able to change languages when they cross the border.

Until recently, children growing up could hardly avoid exposure to elaborated codes. In the media, most characters at least tried to talk like grown-ups, and families sat together and discussed what they saw on the news. Time was spent in talking on other occasions, as well. "Kids used to have to be able to code-switch to talk to their grandparents," commented one linguist. "But the grandparents aren't around the house anymore, and if the parents are home, they seem more willing to switch to the kids' form of talk than to try and force the issue."

Now, for a quantity of hours that exceeds that spent in school, even preadolescents are isolated in their own culture. TV and video talk (if they do at all) either in the teens' own language or in the increasingly agrammatical obfuscations [confusions] of Madison Avenue. With a few notable exceptions, programs rely heavily on picture, gesture, music, and color to get much of the message across. Who needs "talk" containing long clauses, subordinated ideas, and connectives such as "meanwhile," "however," "nevertheless"? Emotionally charged words, not syntax, carry the news. Careful listening becomes irrelevant. Reasoning defers to the surge of immediacy; language use focuses on the literal, the here and now.

Even "literary" models for teenagers are beginning to emphasize the rift with adult culture and its language. In a recent interview, the twenty-five-year-old editor of a new magazine for teenage girls attempted to describe her mission: "Other magazines have, like, a stereotypical or idealized vision of teenagers," she said. "Maybe what parents or teachers would like. Not really what teenagers are about, you know."

School is a foreign country! "It's like, well, you know" does not fly on essay exams. Untrained neural circuits rebel as lectures get longer. Increasingly, students tune out when the teacher talks, avoid literature whenever possible, work silently at their desks or with computer programs, and wait for lunchtime, when they can have a "conversation" that makes sense to them.

Should it be any surprise that when they get to the syntax of Mark Twain, the analytic reasoning of math and science textbooks, or the abstract organization needed to write clearly about something not personal or present, they are lost? Their brains have been molded around language, culture, and thought that are alien, even antagonistic, to those of the school.

QUESTIONS

1. Do you agree that preadolescents are isolated in their own culture? Why or why not?
2. Why might Healy feel that the culture of adolescents is alien to the culture of schools? Do you agree? Why or why not?
3. If adolescents' language development is changing, what impact might this have on our culture as a whole?

Note: Information for cited reference appears in Bibliography. (See page 2.)

From *Endangered Minds* by Jane M. Healy. Copyright © 1990 by Jane M. Healy. Reprinted by permission of *Simon & Schuster*.

CHAPTER

12 ADULTHOOD

Some theorists believe that adulthood follows certain stages. Others believe that there are no predictable life stages. The one thing that seems certain is that most people perform a variety of roles during adulthood, and often they perform two or more of these roles simultaneously for a period of years. Each role that an adult holds comes with its own demands on time, energy, and the adult's identity. Thus, the needs of one role may conflict with the needs of another role. The following excerpt from the book *Family Relations: Challenges for the Future* addresses these issues. This chapter, written by Patricia Voydanoff, was originally presented as part of the Family and Child Studies Center Lecture Series, Miami University, Oxford, Ohio.

The Constraints of Work and Family Roles

Most individuals at some time perform the roles of worker, parent, and/or spouse. Often all of these roles are performed simultaneously. Each involves activities, identities, obligations, and relationships with others. The three roles are interdependent in terms of the time, energy, and commitment required for adequate performance. Under certain circumstances, this interdependence can result in role conflict, a situation in which participation in one role is more difficult because of participation in another role. Role conflict can be of two types, overload and interference. Overload exists when demands on time and energy are too great to be met adequately or comfortably. Interference occurs when conflicting demands make it difficult to fulfill the requirements associated with both work and family roles.

The expectations and demands of work and family roles place constraints on each other over the life course. Traditional work and family roles can be viewed from the perspective of a *career,* defined as a succession of related stages through which persons move in an ordered sequence (Wilensky, 1961). One formulation of occupational career stages includes preparation, novitiate, early career, middle career, late career, and post exit (Bailyn & Schein, 1976). The nature and intensity of work demands vary over these several stages. Some of the most important work influences on family life include amount and scheduling of work time, job demands, orientations to work, and intrinsic work-role characteristics (Voydanoff, 1987).

Families can also be described in terms of career stages such as establishment, new parents, school-aged family, postparental family, and aging family (Hill, 1964). As with work characteristics, several aspects of family roles may be associated with role conflict, for example, family structure (first married, single-parent, or remarried family); presence, number, and ages of children; and the presence of elderly parents needing care.

When individuals pursue traditional work and family role sequences simultaneously, these combined demands frequently result in overload and interference. For example, when individuals in early career stages are also parents of young children, overload is high. In the early stages of a career, individuals are establishing themselves as full members of their occupations, resulting in a relatively high involvement in work (Hall & Hall, 1979). At the same time young children are very demanding in terms of time, attention, and energy (Aldous, 1978). Members of families with young children are likely to experience job tension and a shortage of time. (R. Kelly & Voydanoff, 1985; Voydanoff & Kelly, 1984). Interference tends to be high among families with school-aged children. Timing and scheduling become important as parents are expected to attend school and community functions at times that often conflict with working hours (Harry, 1976). Parents of school-aged children also report high levels of time shortage (Voydanoff & Kelly 1984). In later career stages, work demands require relatively less attention and individuals often have more time for their families. By this time, however, some husbands and wives have developed separate interests and many children have left home (Aldous, 1978; J. Cohen, 1979; Pleck, 1977). Many middle-aged women seeking to establish careers after their children have grown find themselves responsible for the care of elderly parents (E. Brody, 1985).

These patterns of overload and interference have been documented among families in which the husband works outside the home. . . . Until recently most husbands of working wives have spent little, if any, more time in family work than other husbands.

This overload and interference can be reduced on two levels: (a) by individuals and families coordinating their activities so as to limit their work and family role demands and (b) by changes in employment policies and the structure of work.

Individual Responses: Work/Family Role Coordination over the Life Course

Sequential role staging and symmetrical role allocation are two major ways in which individuals and families attempt to reduce the conflicting demands of traditional work and family career patterns. Sequential role staging is used to alternate the work and family responsibilities of the husband and/or wife over the life course. Symmetrical role allocation is an attempt to reduce overload and interference by shifting the responsibilities of work and family roles between the husband and wife within the life course.

QUESTIONS

1. What roles do the adults in your family perform? How might the needs of these roles conflict?

2. The author states that until recently there was no or little difference in the amount of time spent on family chores between husbands with wives who worked outside the home and husbands with wives who did not work outside the home. Do you expect this situation to continue to change? Why or why not?

3. What kinds of skills do you think are useful for a person who must perform multiple roles?

Note: Information for cited references appears in Bibliography. (See page 3.)

From "Constraints of Work and Family Relationships" from *Family Relation: Challenges for the Future* by Timothy H. Brubaker. Copyright © 1993 by *Sage Publications, Inc.* Reprinted by permission of the publisher.

CHAPTER

13

MOTIVATION AND EMOTION

What motivates people to join a group activity or to help a person in need, especially when the group or person in need is unfamiliar to them, is a subject of much psychological study. Some theorists feel that motivation in both instances can be explained by norms, or standards for behavior. In other words, people act the way they do because society has created standards of behavior, which they are motivated to follow. In their book *The Unresponsive Bystander: Why Doesn't He Help?*, Bibb Latané and Jon Darley document a series of experiments they conducted to identify factors that influence people's decisions to participate or not. The excerpt that follows recounts one of those experiments.

To Frisbee or Not To Frisbee

You are probably familiar with the Frisbee, or pluto platter, that appears in the spring. It is a circular, pie plate-like disc which, when propelled by a expert, can be made to fly or float through the air in complex and graceful arcs. The amount of time college students take off from more scholarly activities to devote to the study of Frisbees suggests that the activity is pleasurable and even fascinating. In a study conducted in a senior social psychology seminar at New York University, Sheri Turtletaub and Harriet Ortman cleverly capitalized on this fascination to study the promotion of interaction among groups of strangers. They were concerned with factors promoting interaction among previously nonorganized groups in public places. Most specifically, their task was to turn the Grand Central Station waiting room into a frenzy of flying Frisbees.

A girl sat on a bench in the waiting room at Grand Central. Soon another girl sat on a bench facing her. They recognized each other and began a conversation. One girl had been shopping and announced that she had just bought a Frisbee. The other girl asked to see it and the first girl threw it to her. They then began to toss it back and forth. Apparently by accident, the Frisbee was thrown to a third person and the reaction of this third person (an experimental confederate), was the independent variable of the study. That person either enthusiastically joined in throwing the Frisbee or accused the two girls of being childish and dangerous, and kicked the Frisbee back across the gap.

Whichever of these two variations occurred, the two girls continued throwing the Frisbee back and forth and eventually threw it to one of the real bystanders seated on the benches. They continued this until all the bystanders on the two facing benches had been tried. A bystander was counted as participating in the activity if he returned the Frisbee at least twice. The percentage of bystanders who joined in the Frisbee fest was the dependent measure of the study.

When the experimental confederate joined in the play, the other spectators were extremely likely to do so also. The average percentage of participation over four cases was 86 percent and people often came from other areas of the waiting room to participate. Indeed in this condition the problem was not to start interaction but to terminate it, so the experimenters could leave for the next waiting room and run further tests.

On the other hand, if the confederate refused to play and instead disapproved of the girls' activity, no other bystander ever joined in the action. Instead, people sitting nearby would frequently get up and move to other seats to avoid being thrown a Frisbee, muttering their disapproval while doing so.

The girls went on to run further tests in an attempt to determine which features of the confederate's behavior were critical. In one condition, the confederate returned the Frisbee to the two girls without commenting or otherwise joining in the action. A high percentage, 74 percent, of bystanders participated, not significantly different from the positive participation condition. In another condition, the confederate did not join in the action but allowed the Frisbee to bounce off her accidentally and be retrieved by one of the two original girls. Under these circumstances, too, other bystanders participated at a high rate. The confederate who was a model for inaction failed to inhibit participation by other bystanders.

These results suggest that what the confederate did was less important than what the confederate said. Interaction was significantly inhibited only when the confederate loudly denounced the Frisbee throwers. The results also suggest a normative analysis. When certain norms are made salient, they inhibit action. The experimenters ran other tests to distinguish exactly which norms were operative in the situation. In these further conditions, the confederate carefully confined her negative comments to an appeal to one norm. In one situation, she cited the danger to others that was caused by throwing the Frisbee and in another she accused the participants of indulging in childish behavior.

Both types of sanctions inhibited action about equally. The overall percentage of participation was about 27 percent. However, the girls did a final manipulation which calls a norm-centered account into question: either the confederate stayed to watch the Frisbee players after she gave her sanctions or she immediately left the waiting room. When the confederate stayed, play was greatly inhibited. When she left, the percentage of bystanders participating rose to near its original rate. The sanctioning speech by itself did not inhibit play; it required the sanctioned speech *plus* the confederate's continued presence.

It might be argued that the continued presence of the sanctioning individual made the norm that she had evoked more salient and thus more inhibitory. This, we think, stretches the meaning of the word salience. Even when the denouncer left, she did so only after upbraiding the Frisbee players. Obviously the norms she cited were salient to bystanders, in that they were forcefully brought to their attention. However, the bystanders still participated. Our explanation of the result ignores norms. It seems reasonable that the bystanders simply considered the costs of participating. When the spoilsport confederate stayed around, it was possible that she might yell at other bystanders who participated, call the police, or otherwise punish or embarrass the participants.

QUESTIONS

1. What factors other than norms might have motivated a particular person to either participate or not?
2. Predict your response if the Frisbee were thrown to you. Explain your answer.

From *The Unresponsive Bystander: Why Doesn't He Help* by Bibb Latané and Jon M. Darley. Copyright © 1970 by Meredith Corporation. Reprinted by permission of *Prentice-Hall*, Upper Saddle River, N.J.

CHAPTER

14 THEORIES OF PERSONALITY

Psychologists do not all agree on one particular theory of personality. However, most seem to concur that systems for categorizing personality and classifying people help us make sense of ourselves and others. In his book *The Roots of the Self: Unraveling the Mystery of Who We Are,* noted psychologist and neurobiologist Robert Ornstein discusses the advantages and limits of such classification systems. In the excerpt that follows, Ornstein begins with a recollection of his first introduction to and misunderstanding of Sigmund Freud's theory concerning the id, the ego, and the superego.

It must have been 1947 or 1948.

I was trying to sleep, but my parents had company. My father's friend was explaining some of the theories about the persons that were au courant [current] in postwar New York:

"There's Sid" (I'm still sure that this is what he said), "there's the eagle, and there is the super-eagle, and each of them fights for control."

I knew a Sid who was a friend of my father's, but *this* "Sid" was more like Steve Martin's "wild and crazy kind of guy." The eagle, on the other hand, went forth bravely to organize one's life, while the super-eagle, the super-eagle. Well, I never grasped that one since I got too excited about it. I knew immediately that this was the one I wanted to be. I could see myself soaring over everything. And in my mind, over and over, I could hear the cry:

"Here comes the super-eagle!"

And then there was the inevitable time when I found out I was misinformed about this, and when I also found out the truth about Santa Claus.

Even before this discovery my young mind had made a good case for the usefulness of dividing the person into these three particular parts. Sid, I assumed, tried frantic things, the eagle advanced in life, and when things went wrong there was the amazing super-eagle who would swoop in and save the day.

In retrospect, this concept wasn't so much worse in accounting for the phenomena of the person than many of the more standard divisions of personality. After all, many of the most influential interpretations of the self stem from just such personal conceptions. The thinkers who have become household names may or may not have had professional training, they may or may not have been well informed, and their theories may or may not be functional.

In our own minds, we, too, tend to arrange people into groups, using such categories as excitable, placid, hot, cool, impulsive, disorderly, or controlled. Formal systems use different categories to try to explain individuality, whether those categories include the superego, the "wise old man" or "what's your sign." There must be millions of personality-typing systems, based on everything from skin color to eye color to universal archetypes; the time, day, or date of birth; body type or even blood type; and whether we are choleric, melancholic, Aquarius, introverted, extroverted, or something else.

Ideas for personality classifications, such as id, ego, and superego, may originate from the observations of brilliant scientists. They may come from clinical or biological or casual observation. The theories gain a hold and become part of the language until one knows what to expect from a Leo, an antisocial personality, a redhead . . . or one fixated at the oral stage of development. And these observations and classifications are often interesting and functional. They provide everyone from small children to clinical psychiatrists with a routine for classifying people, one that helps us make sense of ourselves and others.

But that's all they do, since one system doesn't map on to the other, and thus people of different cultures, cults, eras, areas, sciences, and nonsciences have made feeble progress in developing an understanding of the self. The concept of the person can be seen to occupy a "three-dimensional space" (in the mathematical sense), and this space can be filled with almost any three independent assumptions—the vaguer, the better. Personal trouble may mean that the person is possessed by evil spirits, or that a multiple personality is acting up, or the moon is out of joint. We need an explanation to get through the day, and that is what most personality-typing systems provide.

One's own self can't be known in the way one knows one's hair color or height, or even IQ. Human beings do not have, I believe, a "true self" that they can discover by searching through their minds or their experiences. Instead, each person is a composite of the different actions and reactions that come in and out of consciousness as appropriate for any given situation.

And since it is possible to know what is "on our mind" but not what is literally inside it, direct inspection of the self will probably not lead to a true picture. There is a great deal of psychological research that shows that children don't grow up directly knowing what they are thinking. Instead, they, like all of us, make a guess, in part by observing what they are doing and in part by listening to what others say about them. Adults are also rarely able, under careful questioning, to report what is going on inside. We are simply not organized for self-knowledge, no matter how much we'd like to think we are. The mental system, instead, is geared for acting, and self-observation is very difficult.

. . . People find when they observe themselves that their reactions don't follow their preconceived ideas of who they are. They may think of themselves as orderly and serene, for example, but find, after examining their actions, that they are actually driven by excitement, that they have a constant need for stimulation, and that their emotions run the gamut from joy to despair.

QUESTIONS

1. What practical purpose does Ornstein think most personality-typing systems provide?
2. Do you believe that humans have what Ornstein calls a "true self"? Why or why not?
3. Using your own system of categorizing personality and judging from the excerpt, how would you classify the author? Why?

From *"The Puzzle of Individuality"* from *The Roots of The Self* by Robert Ornstein and illustrated by Ted Dewan. Copyright © 1993 by Robert Ornstein. Reprinted by permission of *HarperCollins Publishers, Inc.*

Name ____ Date _______________ Class _______________

PSYCHOLOGICAL TESTS

Early intelligence tests were designed by people who were most familiar with white middle-class culture, and the test questions reflected their background. Psychologists were the first to realize and prove that the low average performance by African Americans on these tests must be attributed to the cultural bias of the test and not—as some erroneously suggested—to a lesser intelligence resulting from genetic inferiority.

In the following excerpt, the author, educational psychologist Martin D. Jenkins, provides evidence that there is virtually no upper limit of ability among African Americans. The excerpt is from a paper that first appeared in *Scientific Monthly* in 1948 and was included in the book *The Psychological Consequences of Being a Black American*. It was praised by author Roger Clark Wilcox as classic and "significant for its having established a more sensible and comprehensive concept of racial intelligence."

More than three decades of psychometric investigation among American Negroes has yielded a rich fund of information concerning this population group. Perhaps the most generally known finding, and certainly the most emphasized, is that when "comparable" groups of whites and Negroes are tested, the Negro group is almost invariably inferior to the whites in psychometric intelligence (intelligence as measured by psychological tests). Preoccupation with the significance of the low *average* performance of Negro groups has served to divert attention from an equally important phenomenon—the variability of the group, and especially the upper limit reached by its really superior members.

The question of the upper limit of ability among Negroes has both theoretical and practical significance. Psychologists generally attribute the low average performance of Negro groups on intelligence tests to cultural factors. It is well known that Negroes generally experience an inferior environment; and there is certainly no question but that an inferior environment tends to depress the psychometric intelligence. There are, however, many Negro children who are nurtured in an environment that is equal or superior to that of the average white child. Thus, we may hypothesize that *if race itself is not a limiting factor in intelligence, then, among Negroes whose total environment compares favorably with that of the average American white, there should be found a "normal" proportion of very superior cases, and the upper limit of ability should coincide with that of the white population.* This hypothesis is especially attractive from a negative aspect; thus, if very superior individuals are not to be found in the Negro population, the environment explanation would clearly be inadequate to account for the phenomenon. The existence of such individuals, on the other hand, would afford additional evidence, but not absolute proof, of course, of the validity of the environmental explanation of racial differences in psychometric intelligence.

The practical significance of the question is apparent. If Negroes are to be found at the highest levels of psychometric intelligence, then we may anticipate that members of this racial group have the ability to participate in the culture at the highest level. In these days of reconsideration of the role of the dark races throughout the world, this question has more than mere national significance.

Analysis of the literature relating to the intelligence-test performance reveals that a considerable number of these children have been found within the range that reaches the best 1 percent of white children (I.Q. 130 and above) and at the level of "gifted" children (I.Q. 140 and above). There are at least sixteen published studies that give an account of Negro children possessing I.Q.s above 130; twelve of these report cases above I.Q. 140. These investigations were made by different psychologists in various localities and under varying conditions; moreover, the I.Q.s were derived by a number of different tests. Further, the populations studied were located almost exclusively in Northern urban communities. Consequently, one may not justifiably generalize, from a composite of these studies, concerning the incidence of Negro deviates. It is of significance, however, that of the 22,301 subjects included in the thirteen studies . . . 0.3 percent scored at I.Q. 130 and above, and fully 1 percent scored at I.Q. 130 and above. These percentages are similar to those obtained from a "normal" I.Q. distribution of American school children.

Of especial significance are the cases of very bright children of Binet I.Q. 160 and above. It may be estimated that fewer than 0.1 percent of school children are to be found at or above this level. As the I.Q. rises above 160 the frequency of occurrence, of course, decreases. Statistically, cases at or above I.Q. 180 should occur about once in a million times, although they actually occur with somewhat greater frequency. In his classic California study of the gifted, Terman found only 15 children testing as high as I.Q. 180; and Hollingworth reports: "In twenty-three years seeking in New York City and the local metropolitan area I have found only twelve children who test at or above 180 I.Q. (Stanford-Binet)." It is apparent then that children who test upwards of Binet I.Q. 160 are extreme deviates in psychometric intelligence and representative of the very brightest children in America.

I have assembled from various scores the case records of 18 Negro children who test above I.Q. 160 on the Stanford-Binet examination. Seven of these cases test above I.Q. 170, 4 above I.Q. 180, and 1 at I.Q. 200. Two of these cases were tested initially by me; the other 16 were reported by psychologists in university centers and public school systems. Analysis of the case records indicates that these children during the early years of development, at least, manifest the same characteristics as do other very high I.Q. children: originality of expression, creative ability, and surpassing performance in school subjects. Some of these children, but not all, are greatly accelerated in school progress. Two, for example, had completed their high-school course and were regularly enrolled university students at age thirteen; both of these subjects were elected to Phi Beta Kappa and earned the baccalaureate degree at age sixteen.

QUESTIONS

1. What, according to the author, is the practical significance of his hypothesis?
2. What does the evidence presented in this excerpt prove?

CHAPTER 16

GENDER ROLES

The roles and responsibilities traditionally assigned to one sex or the other have been increasingly challenged in the last half of the twentieth century. Jobs that once were considered to be the sole territory of males or females are now frequently held by both men and women. Other changes are seen in the assignment of roles in the family. Traditionally, males held jobs outside the home and were the prime source of support for the family. Females stayed home to care for the children. If both parents worked, the needs and demands of the husband's job always superseded those of the wife's job.

In the late 1970s, James Levine researched families that did not follow the traditional assignment of gender roles. The results of his research are presented in his book *Who Will Raise the Children? New Options for Fathers (and Mothers)*. The excerpt that follows summarizes the case of Philip Kramer (false name), who was one of the fathers who made the deliberate choice to stay at home and take care of his children.

Philip Kramer

On Wednesday morning, two days after Sarah Kramer's third birthday, the living room in the large one-bedroom apartment in the Bronx, New York, is still hung with a Happy Birthday banner and crepe-paper streamers. The pigs, goats, and horses from a Fisher Price farmhouse set are grazing on the dark brown carpet, surrounded by "Number-ite," "Speak and Peak," a finger-painting set, and more toys. Across the room, a wall lined with bookshelves holds stacks of the *New York Review of Books* and the *Atlantic Monthly* and thick textbooks. On a low coffee table are some of Sarah's books—*The Sheep Book, Richard Scarry's Best Word Book Ever, Grownups Cry Too.*

On Wednesdays, when Sarah is done watching "Sesame Street," Philip Kramer usually buys fish for dinner. Since the local aquarium store is near the fish market, Philip and Sarah usually stop in to look at the brightly colored fish swimming in their green-blue tanks. They are a familiar couple to most shopkeepers in the neighborhood, known by sight if not by name—Philip, a tall, barrel-chested man whose thick dark beard and balding head make him look older than thirty-three; Sarah, a small golden-haired girl who whisks along in a stroller or prances next to her father's very deliberate stride. Today they have to stop at the bank to deposit the birthday money that Sarah has received from her grandparents, aunts, and uncles. The local branch of the Chase Manhattan has a large open hall with ropes along the sides to guide the customers efficiently into a waiting line.

"Most mothers make their kids stand in line," says Philip. "I let her run. She doesn't really bother anybody." Sarah wanders off to explore the surfaces of the smooth white stones that serve as a decorative base for the bank's two potted plants.

A teenage girl sitting on a nearby bench watches Sarah for a while, then says, "Where's your mother?"

Gail Kramer is in Room 208 at P.S. 83 in the Bronx, a good half hour's subway ride away, teaching English to eleventh graders. It was what she did for six years before Sarah was born, and is what she has done for the last two years since Philip resigned his position as a Legal Aid attorney to stay home with Sarah, then a year old.

"We just did it, we just agreed," offers Gail, indicating how natural it seemed to reverse roles. "I love little kids, but I realized after a year that I'm not the Earth Mother type. I really missed teaching. Philip, at that time, wanted to get some perspective on his job. We're pretty open about our lives. We never planned to do it for more than a year; we try to take things year by year. I don't see how you can plan much further than that."

The Kramers were, however, on what they call a "ten-year plan." Translate: Philip didn't want to have children until after ten years of marriage. In fact, during the first year of Sarah's life, Philip didn't participate at all in the child care. He was literally a father who wouldn't change a diaper.

"When Sarah was four months old, I started to take an African dance class on Monday nights," says Gail, "and Philip was pretty anxious."

With a law degree from Cornell and, ostensibly, not the least inclination to change a diaper, why did Philip Kramer take on full-time fatherhood?

"I did it because it was the right thing to do," says Philip, "I have a very strong sense of justice, and I realized how totally unjust I'd been. Gail wanted to work. Why shouldn't she?" The income difference between Gail's salary as a public-school teacher and Philip's as a Legal Aid attorney—a few thousand dollars—did not alter the situation. "I've never been the sort of person who believed in work. You work if you need money. We won't be rich, but we can live on Gail's salary. Anyway, people have the wrong concept of a lawyer. They think it means someone in an office with clients, making money hand over fist; not someone who is trying to help poor people and who is drawing a salary."

The decision that one parent would stay home with Sarah was never really discussed; it was just assumed. "This isn't the upper west side of Manhattan," says Philip. "Most people around here are very traditional. They yell a lot when there's no need to. They're always treating the kids as if they have less intelligence than they do. We like a strong-willed, self-assertive, self-directing kid. Somebody else might see that as demanding. What was I going to say to someone—let her be free? What does that mean to another person?"

Philip is now in his third year as a full-time father. Because he enjoyed the first year so much, he decided to try another, and then another. When Sarah is four, she will begin attending a day-care center, and Philip Kramer will begin training in early childhood education at Columbia University's Teachers College.

QUESTIONS

1. Levine's book was written in the 1970s. Has much progress been made since then in the acceptance of nontraditional gender roles? What evidence supports your answer?

2. Do you think a man needs to have any particular personality traits to choose to stay home with his children? Why or why not?

3. What do you think are the most important factors in successfully reversing traditional gender roles concerning child care?

From Who Will Raise the Children? *by James A. Levine. Copyright © 1976 by James A. Levine. Reprinted by permission of the author.*

STRESS AND HEALTH

Often people are much more critical of their own appearance than they ever would be of someone else's. Every day people make appointments with cosmetic surgeons hoping to remedy what they consider to be serious problems in their personal appearance. People take this radical step because they are desperate to relieve the anxiety they have developed about how they look. Sometimes that anxiety can be eliminated simply by changing the negative perception rather than the body part. In the excerpts that follow, two writers reveal incidents that changed their perceptions of their faces and led to their adjustment to their situations. These essays first appeared in the June 1996 issue of *The Sun: A Magazine of Ideas.*

Excerpt 1

Terry Atkin Belanger

My mother always told me my face was pretty, but I thought it was too fat. In the first grade, kids started adding an *F* to my last name, calling me Terry "Fatkin." I thought Dad liked my sister better than he liked me, but Mom said it wasn't true. Still, she selected my hairstyles, hats, and headbands on the basis of what would be flattering to a "full" face. (I never understood the distinction between full and fat.) Cute little hats were out because they emphasized the fullness. Short hairstyles didn't work with the round contours. It was best to keep my bangs short or the hair pulled back off my face entirely.

When I was forty-five, I was diagnosed with oral cancer. The lesion was small; doctors only had to remove a third of my tongue and most of the lymph nodes in my neck. The surgeon did a beautiful job, and in a few months I looked pretty much as I had before the operation. I was thrilled and grateful, and I promised God that I would be more gentle with myself, that I wouldn't work so hard, that I would spend quiet time alone, looking within.

Inside me I discovered a shriveled girl, her face drawn and gray. She had been locked away for a long time and was ready to die. I began to try to coax her out. I promised to spend time with her, made every effort to befriend her, to convince her to live.

But life became busy again: work picked up; I remarried; my stepson got married; my son dropped out of college. There were too many things to worry about, and the girl inside me wasn't one of them. Eighteen months after my surgery, I began to notice a tingling and burning in my tongue and mouth. It turned out they hadn't quite gotten all of the cancer.

The second surgery was less kind to my face. This time I lost more of my tongue and more than half of my lower jaw. After seven failed attempts to reconstruct my jaw out of bone from my hip, the surgeons used a titanium bar and tissue from my left breast and my chest wall to rebuild my mouth. Sutures paraded up and down my side, converging on my mouth, neck, and chin. After the operation, I asked that the mirrors in my hospital room be covered with get-well cards and pictures.

It has been three years since that surgery, and I still avoid mirrors and the direct gaze of children. Strangers' eyes linger on my face for a moment too long, But the neglected girl inside me has emerged and can come and go as she pleases. We like to wear long bangs and hats of all sizes.

Excerpt 2

Jennifer Yeo

The driver, in despair over his recent divorce, had mixed painkillers before he ran the traffic light and collided with our VW bus. My face smashed into the dashboard, shattering my jaw in seven places. I was almost four years old, too young for surgery, so the doctors cut off my hair, wrapped my head in bandages, and told my parents to "wait and see."

At first, it seemed the only visible reminder of the accident would be a small scar from the stitches, cleverly tucked under my chin. But as I grew, something wasn't quite right: my face was lopsided. Doctors theorized that a "growth center" had been traumatized by the accident, and that as a result the left side of my jaw had developed normally while the right side had remained small and childlike.

As a teenager, I cursed my appearance, until gradually I realized that only dentists and photographers could tell my jaw was slightly askew. To others, my face had an exotic quality they couldn't quite put their finger on.

Later in life, after my divorce, my ex-husband's parting salvo—"I no longer find you attractive"—haunted me. I began to obsess about my minor facial flaw, thinking it the source of my problems, and came to believe that correcting it would restore my happiness. I consulted an oral surgeon, who sent photographs of me to a special lab where a computer adjusted my image to show how I might took after the ordeal of surgery and a year of braces. The doctor was confident that I would take one look at these before-and-after photos and immediately begin preparations for the procedure.

I looked from one to the other: the now me and the postsurgery me. I found the perfect, symmetrical future face boring. Not ugly, not beautiful; just bland. I left the surgeon's office, thrilled with my interesting, extraordinary face.

QUESTIONS

1. What was the catalyst of perception change in each excerpt?
2. What might really have been the source of Yeo's problem when she began to think her minor facial flaw was a fault?
3. Have you ever suddenly changed your perception of a personal body feature or of another person? Explain your answer.

From "Readers Write: Faces" by Jennifer Yeo from *The Sun,* June 1996. Copyright © 1996 by Jennifer Yeo. Reprinted by permission of the author.

CHAPTER

18 · PSYCHOLOGICAL DISORDERS

Major depression is a mental disorder that triggers pervasive and very strong feelings of fear, helplessness, sadness, and isolation. In some cases, these feelings become so overwhelming that the person who is depressed may mistakenly feel that suicide is the only way to stop the pain. In his book *Darkness Visible: A Memoir of Madness,* noted author William Styron recounts his own descent into the despair of major depression beginning in the summer of 1985 and his unsteady but triumphant climb back to health. Three excerpts from that book appear below.

Excerpt 1

By now I had moved back to my house in Connecticut. It was October, and one of the unforgettable features of this stage of my disorder was the way in which my own farmhouse, my beloved home for thirty years, took on for me at that point when my spirits regularly sank to their nadir [lowest point] an almost palpable quality of ominousness. The fading evening light—akin to that famous "slant of light" of Emily Dickinson's, which spoke to her of death, of chill extinction—had none of its familiar autumnal loveliness, but ensnared me in a suffocating gloom. I wondered how this friendly place, teeming with such memories of (again in her words) "Lads and Girls," of "laughter and ability and Sighing, / And Frocks and Curls," could almost perceptibly seem so hostile and forbidding. Physically, I was not alone. As always Rose was present and listened with unflagging patience to my complaints. But I felt an immense and aching solitude. I could no longer concentrate during those afternoon hours, which for years had been my working time, and the act of writing itself, becoming more and more difficult and exhausting, stalled, then finally ceased.

There were also dreadful, pouncing seizures of anxiety. One bright day on a walk through the woods with my dog I heard a flock of Canada geese honking high above trees ablaze with foliage; ordinarily a sight and sound that would have exhilarated me, the flight of birds caused me to stop, riveted with fear, and I stood stranded there, helpless, shivering, aware for the first time that I had been stricken by no mere pangs of withdrawal but by a serious illness whose name and actuality I was able finally to acknowledge. Going home, I couldn't rid my mind of the line of Baudelaire's, dredged up from the distant past, that for several days had been skittering around at the edge of my consciousness: "I have felt the wind of the wing of madness."

Excerpt 2

November wore on, bleak, raw and chill. One Sunday a photographer and his assistants came to take pictures for an article to be published in a national magazine. Of the session I can recall little except the first snowflakes of winter dotting the air outside. I thought I obeyed the photographer's request to smile often. A day or two later the magazine's editor telephoned my wife, asking if I would submit to another session. The reason he advanced was that the pictures of me, even the ones with smiles, were "too full of anguish."

I had now reached that phase of the disorder where all sense of hope had vanished, along with the idea of a futurity; my brain, in thrall to its outlaw hormones, had become less an organ of thought than an instrument registering, minute by minute, varying degrees of its own suffering. The mornings themselves were becoming bad now as I wandered about lethargic, following my synthetic sleep, but afternoons were still the worst, beginning at about three o'clock, when I'd feel the horror, like some poisonous fogbank, roll in upon my mind, forcing me into bed. There I would lie for as long as six hours, stuporous and virtually paralyzed, gazing at the ceiling and waiting for that moment of evening when, mysteriously, the crucifixion would ease up just enough to allow me to force down some food and then, like an automaton, seek an hour or two of sleep again. Why wasn't I in a hospital?

Excerpt 3

By far the great majority of the people who go through even the severest depression survive it, and live ever afterward at least as happily as their unafflicted counterparts. Save for the awfulness of certain memories it leaves, acute depression inflicts few permanent wounds. There is a Sisyphean torment in the fact that a great number—as many as half—of those who are devastated once will be struck again; depression has the habit of recurrence. But most victims live through even these relapses, often coping better because they have become psychologically tuned by past experience to deal with the ogre. It is of great importance that those who are suffering a siege, perhaps for the first time, be told—be convinced, rather—that the illness will run its course and that they will pull through. A tough job, this; calling "Chin up!" from the safety of the shore to a drowning person is tantamount to insult, but it has been shown over and over again that if the encouragement is dogged enough—and the support equally committed and passionate—the endangered one can nearly always be saved. Most people in the grip of depression at its ghastliest are, for whatever reason, in a state of unrealistic hopelessness, torn by exaggerated ills and fatal threats that bear no resemblance to actuality. It may require on the part of friends, lovers, family, admirers, an almost religious devotion to persuade the sufferers of life's worth, which is so often in conflict with a sense of their own worthlessness, but such devotion has prevented countless suicides.

During the same summer of my decline, a close friend of mine—a celebrated newspaper columnist—was hospitalized for severe manic depression. By the time I had commenced my autumnal plunge my friend had recovered (largely due to lithium but also to psychotherapy in the aftermath), and we were in touch by telephone nearly every day. His support was untiring and priceless. It was he who kept admonishing me that suicide was "unacceptable" (he had been intensely suicidal), and it was also he who made the prospect of going to the hospital less fearsomely intimidating. I still look back on his concern with immense gratitude. The help he gave me, he later said, had been a continuing therapy for him, thus demonstrating that, if nothing else, the disease engenders lasting fellowship.

QUESTIONS

1. In excerpt 1, what evidence is there that Styron's knowledge of literature is prominent in his consciousness?

2. In excerpt 2, do you think that the time of the year contributed to Styron's depression? Why or why not?

3. What could you do if you suspected that a friend or family member had major depression?

From *Darkness Visible: A Memoir of Madness* by William Styron. Copyright © 1990 by William Styron. Reprinted by permission of *Random House, Inc.*

CHAPTER 19
METHODS OF THERAPY

The psychotherapies of a culture reflect ways of looking at people and their problems that are consistent with the philosophies and perceptions of that culture. For example, in most Western therapies, anxiety is an intrusive element, a symptom, comparable to a fever or a rash. The goal of Western psychotherapy is to rid the patient of the symptom. In Morita psychotherapy—developed by Japanese philosopher-psychiatrist Morita Shoma in the early 1900s—patients are taught to see their anxiety as a part of themselves rather than as an appended symptom. The goal of Morita psychotherapy is to help patients become so involved in the needs of the moment that they lose awareness of the part of them that is the "anxiety." Although Morita psychotherapy contains some ideas from Western psychotherapies, it is predominately saturated with Japanese thought and, therefore, has a distinct Japanese character.

A major treatment pattern in Morita psychotherapy is to begin with a week of isolated bed rest and then to gradually reintroduce the patient back to social interaction and productive work. Patients keep a diary during treatment. The following excerpt is from a case history of an adolescent patient in treatment. The excerpt is from the book *The Quiet Therapies* by David K. Reynolds, who studied Morita by experiencing it and who eventually applied it in his own practice.

Case Histories

Case 1. A seventeen-year-old male high school student. This patient's chief complaints were a lack of ability to talk with people comfortably, distraction of attention, insomnia, intense inferiority feelings, and becoming easily fatigued.

Diary opening: "I am nervous by nature. I hear that when I was a baby I used to cry out frightened by any little sound. Since I was a child I have suffered greatly from feelings of isolation, humiliation, and suspicion at home and at school. In my early teens I had already developed many of my symptoms and distortion of character. Now I am bothered by anthropophobia [fear of people], low efficiency, timidity, anxiety, insomnia, fatigue, as well as such persistent difficulties as . . . inferiority feelings, difficulty in concentrating, [facial] tics, body tremors, and a fear of sudden noises. Can someone like me really be helped by Morita therapy? If I find relief it will be a miracle."

First day after absolute bed rest: "I left my bed for the first time. But everyone here is unfamiliar and I am not thinking clearly. When my symptoms emerged as usual, I worried about them alone in my room. After lunch I began to get accustomed to the people's faces, met some people, and worked a little. But I felt anxious about their eyes, as I've felt before. Although the doctor said in his lecture that there is no need to be a great man, I still have an earnest desire to be great. Even now I intend to conquer my neurosis through Morita therapy and then to improve my personality through Zen or yoga. Yet I'm afraid this intention is wrong. Certainly, when I am in a group I enter into rivalry with the others. What a fix I am in! Furthermore, since I am very clumsy how will I be able to do the handicrafts? If I do, my work will be worthless. I am completely lacking in self-assurance. But today's harvest was that by not running away I was able to establish friendly relations with almost all the people here by evening."

Seventh day: "This is the most painful time for me. I must get through this period at any cost and advance toward the future. I am such a contradictory being. I am caught in a circle and cannot stir an inch. Last night I dreamed that I was caught in the web of a gigantic spider. The spider came and said to me, 'It's no use struggling. You can't escape.' The dream reflected my present state of mind. Now I am beginning to look on the bright side of things. If I do as the doctor tells me I will gain something at least, however trifling the gain is. I will let things take their own course."

Thirty-third day: "I filled the oil heater. This was my first time doing it, so I couldn't do it very well. When I finished my hands were stained with oil. Took care of the birds. Today a lovebird egg hatched, two days late. Next I cleaned the garden. Read. Played Ping-Pong. Then I saw my mother off at Takatanobaba Station. I had my watch repaired in a watchmaker's shop. Although I had to struggle with myself to enter the shop, I opened the door in spite of my apprehension. After supper I was visited by Mr. A., a former patient here, and we went into Shinjuku to buy books and have a snack. It was pleasant to see Mr. A. again—it seems so long ago that he was discharged. I felt some self-consciousness, but everything went well. Then I picked up my watch at the watchmaker's shop. Then I delivered a book that I had earlier promised to lend to a fellow patient. She was in the hospital's craftsroom with a number of other women. I have a strong desire to be respected and loved, which is one of the characteristics of anthropophobia. According to Morita therapy I should recognize this strong desire and accept and use it rather than focusing on my symptoms. But I fear that if I do so I will become passive, stereotypic, and artificial."

Forty-eighth day: "Today I shall end my diary at Koseiin Clinic. I am filled with emotion. I have gradually come to understand the word *arugamama* [accepting one's self, one's symptoms, and reality as they are; lit., "as it is"]. No matter what my ideals, ideas, and feelings may be, it is most important to accept reality. In fact, I can't help responding to reality. Looking at it one way, I am thankful for having been an anthropophobic patient. I have advanced one step, and now I want to go on advancing endlessly. In sum, I dimly begin to realize that this neurosis was like a springboard which enabled me to develop myself. I desire to understand myself fully and then to use that knowledge in a practical way. Thanks to my mastery of life through Morita therapy, I have become aware of my true self now. I find it gratifying that my true self is not so much inferior as it is great. I really thank you for your long-range guidance." (Ohara and Reynolds, n.d.)

QUESTIONS

1. In one sentence, summarize the lesson that the patient learned.
2. What evidence is there of the patient's feelings toward his doctor?
3. Do you think the patient is cured? Why or why not?

Note: Information for cited reference appears in Bibliography. (See page 3.)

From *The Quiet Therapies: Japanese Pathways to Personal Growth* by David K. Reynolds. Copyright © 1980 by the *University of Hawaii Press.* Reprinted by permission of the publisher.

CHAPTER

20

READING

SOCIAL COGNITION

Principles of Psychology—published in 1890—is considered the first modern psychology text. Its author, William James (1842-1910), is hailed as a major figure in the development of American psychology. James founded a school of psychology called functionalism. The thinking of this school was that a person's specific psychological processes—behaviors, thoughts, and emotions—must serve a purpose for the person, or the processes would be changed or lost.

The excerpt that follows is from *Psychology,* James' abridged version of *Principles of Psychology,* which he published in 1892. In the excerpt, he discusses the role of the surrounding society in determining an individual's perceptions, reasons, emotions, and actions.

The Social Me—A man's social me is the recognition which he gets from his mates. We are not only gregarious animals, liking to be in sight of our fellows, but we have an innate propensity to get ourselves noticed, and noticed favorably, by our kind. No more fiendish punishment could be devised, were such a thing physically possible, than that one should be turned loose in society and remain absolutely unnoticed by all the members thereof. If no one turned round when we entered, answered when we spoke, or minded what we did, but if every person we met "cut us dead," and acted as if we were non-existing things, a kind of rage and impotent despair would ere [before] long well up in us, from which the cruelest bodily tortures would be a relief; for these would make us feel that, however bad might be our plight, we had not sunk to such a depth as to be unworthy of attention at all.

Properly speaking, a man has as many social selves as there are individuals who recognize him and carry an image of him in their mind. To wound any one of these his images is to wound him. But as the individuals who carry the images fall naturally into classes, we may practically say that he has as many different social selves as there are distinct *groups* of persons about whose opinion he cares. He generally shows a different side of himself to each of these different groups. Many a youth who is demure enough before his parents and teachers, swears and swaggers like a pirate among his "tough" young friends. We do not show ourselves to our children as to our club-companions, to our customers as to the laborers we employ, to our own masters and employers as to our intimate friends. From this there results what practically is a division of the man into several selves; and this may be a discordant splitting, as where one is afraid to let one set of his acquaintances know him as he is elsewhere; or it may be a perfectly harmonious division of labor, as where one tender to his children is stern to the soldiers or prisoners under his command.

The most peculiar social self which one is apt to have is in the mind of the person one is in love with. The good or bad fortunes of this self cause the most intense elation and dejection—unreasonable enough as measured by every other standard than that of the organic feeling of the individual. To his own consciousness he is not, so long as this particular social self fails to get recognition, and when it is recognized his contentment passes all bounds.

A man's *fame,* good or bad, and his *honor* or dishonor, are names for one of his social selves. The particular social self of a man called his honor is usually the result of one of those splittings of which we have spoken. It is his image in the eyes of his own "set," which exalts or condemns him as he conforms or not to certain requirements that may not be made of one in another walk of life. Thus a layman may abandon a city infected with cholera; but a priest or a doctor would think such an act incompatible with his honor. A soldier's honor requires him to fight or to die under circumstances where another man can apologize or run away with no stain upon his social self. A judge, a statesman, are in like manner debarred by the honor of their cloth from entering into pecuniary [monetary] relations perfectly honorable to persons in private life. Nothing is commoner than to hear people discriminate between their different selves of this sort: "As a man I pity you, but as an official I must show you no mercy"; "As a politician I regard him as an ally, but as a moralist I loathe him"; etc., etc. What may be called "club-opinion" is one of the very strongest forces in life. The thief must not steal from other thieves; the gambler must pay his gambling-debts, though he pay no other debts in the world. The code of honor of fashionable society has throughout history been full of permissions as well as of vetoes, the only reason for following either of which is so that we best serve one of our social selves. You must not lie in general but you may lie as much as you please if asked about your relations with a lady; you must accept a challenge from an equal, but if challenged by an inferior you may laugh him to scorn: these are examples of what is meant.

QUESTIONS

1. Do you think James' description of the influence of society on human behavior is still valid today? Why or why not?

2. What evidence have you observed that people have more than one social self?

3. Do you agree with James' statement that "the most peculiar social self which one is apt to have is in the mind of the person one is in love with"? Why or why not?

21

SOCIAL INTERACTION

In his book *The Saturated Self,* Kenneth J. Gergen, professor of psychology at Swarthmore College, suggests that as expanding communication technologies invade more and more aspects of modern life, people are forced to interact with far more people on a daily basis than was common in the past. Gergen calls our condition social saturation. In the excerpt that follows, he explores the effect of social saturation on forming and maintaining friendships in today's society.

A century ago, social relationships were largely confined to the distance of an easy walk. Most were conducted in person, within small communities: family, neighbors, townspeople. Yes, the horse and carriage made longer trips possible, but even a trip of thirty miles could take all day. The railroad could speed one away, but cost and availability limited such travel. If one moved from the community, relationships were likely to end. From birth to death one could depend on relatively even-textured social surroundings. Words, faces, gestures, and possibilities were relatively consistent, coherent, and slow to change.

For much of the world's population, especially the industrialized West, the small, face-to-face community is vanishing into the pages of history. We go to country inns for weekend outings, we decorate condominium interiors with clapboards and brass beds, and we dream of old age in a rural cottage. But as a result of the technological developments just described, contemporary life is a swirling sea of social relations. Words thunder in by radio, television, newspaper, mail, telephone, fax, wire service, electronic mail, billboards, Federal Express, and more. Waves of new faces are everywhere—in town for a day, visiting for the weekend, at the Rotary lunch, at the church social—and incessantly and incandescently [glowingly] on television. Long weeks in a single community are unusual; a full day within a single neighborhood is becoming rare. We travel casually across town, into the countryside, to neighboring towns, cities, states; one might go thirty miles for coffee and conversation.

Through the technologies of the century, the number and variety of relationships in which we are engaged, potential frequency of contact, expressed intensity of relationship, and endurance through time all are steadily increasing. As this increase becomes extreme we reach a state of social saturation. Let us consider this state in greater detail.

In the face-to-face community the cast of others remained relatively stable. There were changes by virtue of births and deaths, but moving from one town—much less state or country—to another was difficult. The number of relationships commonly maintained in today's world stands in stark contrast. Counting one's family, the morning television news, the car radio, colleagues on the train, and the local newspaper, the typical commuter may confront as many different persons (in terms of views or images) in the first two hours of a day as the community-based predecessor did in a month. The morning calls in a business office may connect one to a dozen different locales in a given city, often across the continent, and very possibly across national boundaries. A single hour of prime-time melodrama immerses one in the lives of a score of individuals. In an evening of television, hundreds of engaging faces insinuate themselves into our lives. It is not only the immediate community that occupies our thoughts and feelings, but a constantly changing cast of characters spread across the globe.

Two aspects of this expansion are particularly noteworthy. First there is what may be termed the *perseverance of the past.* Formerly, increases in time and distance between persons typically meant loss. When someone moved away, the relationship would languish. Long-distance visits were arduous, and the mails slow. Thus, as one grew older, many active participants would fade from one's life. Today, time and distance are no longer such serious threats to a relationship. One may sustain an intimacy over thousands of miles by frequent telephone raptures punctuated by occasional visits. One may similarly retain relationships with high-school chums, college roommates, old military cronies, or friends from a Caribbean vacation five years earlier. Birthday books have become a standard household item; one's memory is inadequate to record the festivities for which one is responsible. In effect, as we move through life, the cast of relevant characters is ever expanding. For some this means an everincreasing sense of stress: "How can we make friends with them? We don't even have time for the friends we already have!" For others there is a sense of comfort, for the social caravan in which we travel through life remains always full.

Yet at the same time that the past is preserved, continuously poised to insert itself into the present, there is an *acceleration of the future.* The pace of relationships is hurried, and processes of unfolding that once required months or years may be accomplished in days or weeks. A century ago, for example, courtships were often carried out on foot or horseback, or through occasional letters. Hours of interchange might be punctuated by long periods of silence, making the path from acquaintanceship to intimacy lengthy. With today's technologies, however, it is possible for a couple to maintain almost continuous connection. Not only do transportation technologies chip away at the barrier of geographic distance, but through telephone (both stable and cordless), overnight mail, cassette recordings, home videos, photographs, and electronic mail, the other may be "present" at almost any moment. Courtships may thus move from excitement to exhaustion within a short time. The single person may experience not a handful of courtship relationships in a lifetime but dozens. In the same way, the process of friendship is often accelerated. Through the existing technologies, a sense of affinity may blossom into a lively sense of interdependence within a brief space of time. As the future opens, the number of friendships expands as never before.

QUESTIONS

1. With which of the two described possible reactions to the ever-expanding cast of relevant characters in a person's life might you identify?

2. Do you feel that your lifestyle supports Gergen's theories on friendships? Explain your answer.

From "The Process of Social Saturation" from *The Saturated Self* by Kenneth J. Gergen. Copyright © 1991 by *Basic Books, a division of HarperCollins Publishers, Inc.*

Answers

7 Chapter

1. According to Standard 8.05, psychologists may dispense with informed consent when (1) research would not reasonably be assumed to create distress or harm or (2) where otherwise permitted by law or federal or institutional regulations.

2. According to Standard 8.06, psychologists should make reasonable efforts to avoid offering excessive or inappropriate financial or other inducements for research participation. Students may offer differing opinions on whether participants should be paid. Accept answers that are logically supported.

3. According to Standard 8.07, psychologists should not deceive prospective participants about research that is reasonably expected to cause physical pain or severe emotional distress.

2 Chapter

1. Mimetic signs that automatically transmit a certain mood have undoubtedly degenerated as our word-language has developed. *Sample answer:* It is likely that Lorenz's field observations contributed to his conclusions about mimetic signs.

2. Students may describe a behavior signal of a household pet.

3. Students may describe minute signals that can convey complex information between people who have a close bond.

3 Chapter

1. John Dechow's motor skills were noticeably less affected than his mental skills.

2. John Dechow especially appreciated his son Paul's willingness to listen.

3. *Sample answer:* It is difficult for family members to witness the behavior changes brought on by Alzheimer's disease because the disease changes a person to such an extent that he or she seems a different person. The family members feel they have lost their loved one, even though he or she is still there.

4 Chapter

1. Because of their own experiences, most students will agree with Krueger that sight is the dominant sense.

2. Students may relate a theme park ride or being seated on a stationary train or bus while observing a similar vehicle moving beside them as an example of when their vision momentarily overruled their reason.

3. Students may argue that perceptions that people have while in an artificial-reality environment are real because they are true to the environment that they are in and because the body reacts to the perceptions as it would to "real" ones. Students may also argue that only perceptions true to the actual world are real.

Chapter 5

1. Dement identifies the discovery of REM sleep as the breakthrough discovery in sleep research.

2. A good case can be made for crediting the sleep research team as equal partners in the discovery of REM sleep. Some students may feel that Eugene Aserinsky, who first noticed the rapid eye movements, deserves credit. Although William Dement coined the term, he was not the first to discover the phenomenon.

3. No, because of Dement's statement that "there is nothing more exciting to a researcher than findings that are totally different from what he expected."

Chapter 6

1. In one of the two cultural patterns of speech researchers have identified, caregivers simplify their talk, negotiate meaning with children, and respond to their verbal and nonverbal initiations. In the other pattern, caregivers model unsimplified utterances for children to repeat to a third party, direct them to notice others, and build interaction around circumstances to which the caregivers wish the children to respond.

2. The first pattern mentioned is typical of middle-class U.S. families. Examples include use of the term the child uses for something rather than the correct term in conversations with the child.

3. *Sample answers:* Yes, because everyone else talks that way to them..No, I think it is important to model correct speech.

Chapter 7

1. In most cases, people are not aware of their mind's distortions of events.

2. Eyewitness testimony is convincing because people in general believe that memories stamp the facts of our experiences on a permanent, nonerasable tape, like a computer disk or videotape that is write-protected.

3. *Sample answers:* Yes, because it is a storage place where individual pieces can be filed, moved, refiled, misfiled, and lost. No, because memories are not stored as complete, intact events.

Chapter 8

1. undirected thought and directed thought

2. because psychologists do not know how to probe the private nature of undirected thought without seriously disturbing it.

3. comprehension, memory, generation of ideas, evaluation of ideas, implementation, and occasionally public report

9 Chapter

1. According to the article, intelligence tests actually are more successful at measuring a type of practiced learning and familiarity with the test questions than they are at measuring innate, immutable intelligence. Therefore, one would expect children with no formal schooling to do poorly on a standard IQ test.

2. *Sample answer:* Practice in working with models of the test-question format, including mazes and mental paper folding, will best help students prepare for an IQ test.

3. *Sample answers:* Yes, because everyone takes the same test and it is a way of sorting people. No, because of cultural bias. No, because it has been proved that the tests do not test immutable intelligence.

10 Chapter

1. *Sample answer:* Children may become more concerned with reality as they mature because society seems to require that people set aside fantasy and make-believe along with their childish toys as part of growing up.

2. *Sample answer:* The availability of software that facilitates the creation of artificial worlds may motivate more children to create make-believe worlds, but their creativity will be limited by the scope of the software.

3. Answers depend on personal experience.

11 Chapter

1. *Sample answers:* Yes, because they spend the most time with peers. No, because they are exposed to a wide variety of ideas by people of all ages through the media.

2. The culture of adolescents may be alien to the culture of Healy, and she associates her own culture with being compatible with the school environment. *Sample answers:* Yes, because the school environment is closely related to the work environment. No, because the culture of adolescents is part of the school environment.

3. As today's adolescents mature, they will affect the culture of, first, the young adult population of society, then the middle-aged adult population, and finally, the elderly adults. In time, nursing homes will be filled with people communicating through statements such as, "Like, so I goes."

12 Chapter

1. *Sample answer:* Parent, daughter, editor, student. The time, energy, and commitment of the various roles may conflict.

2. *Sample answers:* Yes, because more and more women are working outside the home. No, because the designation to work within the home as woman's work is too ingrained in some family cultures.

3. *Sample answer:* Organizational skills, time-management skills, and stress-control skills are examples of skills useful to a person who must fulfill multiple roles.

Chapter 13

1. *Sample answer:* An individual's current frame of mind or physical condition might have been the real determining factor in whether he or she would participate or not.

2. Answer will depend on individual personalities.

Chapter 14

1. Ornstein suggests that personality classification systems provide us with a routine for classifying people in a way that helps us make sense of ourselves and others.

2. Answers depend on personal definitions of "true self."

3. Answers depend on personal systems of categorizing personalities. Students should be able to give evidence from the excerpt that supports the general definition of the personality type they assign to the author.

Chapter 15

1. The practical significance of the author's hypothesis is that if African Americans are to be found at the highest levels of psychometric intelligence, then we may anticipate that members of this racial group have the ability to participate in the culture at the highest level.

2. *Sample answer:* The evidence presented in this excerpt proves that race is not a limiting factor in intelligence.

Chapter 16

1. *Sample answer:* Yes. Jobs such as nurse, firefighter, construction worker, and physician, once considered the sole territory for males, are now successfully filled by both males and females.

2. *Sample answer:* Yes. Men who supervise young children need to have a patient, gentle, nurturing personality. No. It is tradition that requires certain traits of those who supervise young children. The children will do just as well with anyone who has their best interest at heart.

3. *Sample answer:* an open mind, a flexible attitude, and a strong sense of self

Chapter 17

1. For the first excerpt, the catalyst of perception change was cancer surgery that caused a pronounced disfigurement. For the second excerpt, the catalyst was a glimpse into how a wished-for physical change would actually appear.

2. *Sample answer:* a general loss of self-esteem caused by her husband's malicious remark and the breakup of her marriage

3. Answers will vary. Be sure students explain their answers.

Chapter 18

1. Styron easily draws on the works of Emily Dickinson and Charles Baudelaire to find the words to describe his feelings at this time.

2. *Sample answer:* Yes, because weather conditions during November in Connecticut can be bleak—little sunshine, frequent gray skies and freezing drizzle or snow.

3. *Sample answer:* continually encourage the person by reminding him or her that the illness will run its course and that he or she will pull through

Chapter 19

1. *Sample answer:* It is important to face up to reality.

2. *Sample answers:* Although he had many doubts about his own ability in the beginning, the patient carried out all the orders of the doctor without question. Also, the patient ended his diary with a sincere thank-you.

3. *Sample answer:* No, because he still exhibits some of the same qualities for which he entered Morita psychotherapy. However, he is now able to accept the reality of those qualities.

Chapter 20

1. *Sample answer:* Yes, because people tend to modify their behavior, depending on their current social environment.

2. *Sample answers:* talking to friends outside of class and seeing their actions in class; a person acting in a group in a manner that is quite different from how the person acts when he or she is alone with you

3. Answers will depend on personal experiences and observation.

Chapter 21

1. Answers will depend on individual personalities.

2. Answers will depend on individual personalities.

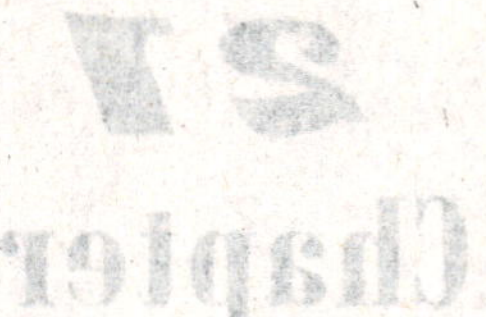